YVES R. SIMON

Twentieth-Century Political Thinkers

Series Editors: Kenneth L. Deutsch and Jean Bethke Elshtain

YVES R. SIMON

Real Democracy

VUKAN KUIC

ROWMAN & LITTLEFIELD PUBLISHERS, INC.
Lanham • Boulder • New York • Oxford

ROWMAN & LITTLEFIELD PUBLISHERS, INC.

Published in the United States of America
by Rowman & Littlefield Publishers, Inc.
4720 Boston Way, Lanham, Maryland 20706
http://www.rowmanlittlefield.com

12 Hid's Copse Road
Cumnor Hill, Oxford OX2 9JJ, England

British Library Cataloguing in Publication Information Available

Library of Congress Cataloging-in-Publication Data

Kuic, Vukan.
    Yves R. Simon : real democracy / Vukan Kuic.
        p.   cm. — (Twentieth-century political thinkers)
    Includes bibliographical references and index.
    ISBN 0-8476-9612-X (alk. paper). — ISBN 0-8476-9613-8 (pbk. :
alk. paper)
        1. Simon, Yves René Marie, 1903–1961—Contributions in political
science.   I. Title.   II. Title: Real democracy   III. Series.
JC261.S58K85   1999
320'.092—dc21   99-16270
                                                      CIP

Printed in the United States of America

∞ ™ The paper used in this publication meets the minimum requirements of
American National Standard for Information Sciences—Permanence of Paper
for Printed Library Materials, ANSI/NISO Z39.48–1992.

CONTENTS

And so too, it seems should one make a return to those with whom one has studied philosophy . . . they can get no honor which will balance their services, but it is perhaps enough . . . to give them what one can.

Ethics 1164^{b}2–7

1

PHILOSOPHER IN THE CITY

Yves R. Simon was not a political scientist nor even primarily a political philosopher. He was, however, a profound thinker, and, faithful to the tradition of Western philosophy, he understood well the need for continuous reexamination of mankind's political experience from a philosophical point of view. Simon wrote his doctoral dissertation on the metaphysics of knowledge and in the same year published also a monograph on moral knowledge.[1] But in 1936, "an immensely sad event," as he put it, gave him "a chance to come out as a political writer." Denouncing the Italian invasion of Ethiopia, Simon traced its contributing factors to widespread hypocrisy, worship of force, disregard for law and treatises, and shameful exploitation of wicked instincts, to all of which he found accomplices among many French intellectuals.[2] Interestingly enough, a few years later Simon regretted preserving in this book "the serenity of expression, the abstractness, and politeness which become a philosopher"—all other things being equal.[3] But as the world situation deteriorated from scandalous to catastrophic, Simon adjusted his style accordingly. He had come to the United States, the Second World War had broken out, and in 1941 Simon joined the cause of the Free French with a passionate condemnation of all whom he held responsible for the collapse of France. He exposed by name a number of "moral gangsters," both of the left and of the right, including members of the Catholic hierarchy.[4] Yet ever more political philosopher than activist, Simon in the same year wrote also another book in which he urged that the day of liberation be also the day of reconciliation in a reborn French Fourth Republic.[5] And as the big war finally ended, he was inspired to publish his last political tract, in which he specified some general principles and conditions for the kind of world that in his opin-

1

ion would justify the sacrifices endured.[6] Almost forty years later, this small book has been found worthy of being reprinted, because as one reviewer explains it,

> Simon's way of treating his subject makes his book readily applicable to social situations that have occurred much later. The concrete conditions that led to his reflections do not dominate the content of these reflections; rather the concrete gave Simon the occasion to construct arguments of principle and generality that live on. It is not only possible but, in this reviewer's opinion, very beneficial to ponder these essays with the news of the 1980's as a factual accompaniment. *The Community of the Free* has transcended the era that saw its birth.[7]

Indeed, what most commentators have routinely praised in Simon's writings is their timeless quality. Thus reviewing one of Simon's posthumous volumes dealing with the broad subject of the relation between work and culture, Hans Morgenthau puts it this way:

> Reading this book, one is struck by one quality which distinguishes the whole of Simon's work: the combination of profound understanding of the basic insights of Western philosophy with a vivid experience of the philosophic problems of the contemporary world. It is the interaction of these two factors which is at the root of Simon's originality and importance for contemporary philosophy. It must also be said in favor of this book that, while it is closely reasoned, it is easily accessible to the reader. Since the author is telling us something which is worth listening to, he does not need to resort to a jargon, which only too often fills an intellectual void with the appearance of inaccessible profundity.[8]

These evaluations of Simon's later work confirm the judgment of a scholar of authority and reputation who reviewed Simon's doctoral dissertation. That earliest reviewer praised Simon, who had just passed the age of thirty, not just for daring to enter a field which most other philosophers would rather avoid, i.e., the metaphysics of knowledge, but also for his distinct style: "He boldly recognizes the difficulties," Louis de Raeymaeker wrote, "and one cannot help but admire the precision of his formulation of the problems and the tight dialectic of his exposition and solutions."[9] And thirty-five years later, in the foreword to yet another of Simon's posthumous books, Mortimer Adler expanded that evaluation in a breathless paragraph-long sentence as follows:

> This book, as I have said, is the perfect antidote for the errors, the misunderstandings—or worse, the ignorances—that beset the modern discussion of free choice. Even a reader who comes to this book with little or no knowledge of the philosophical literature on the subject that it treats cannot fail to appreciate its remarkable clarity, its felicitous combination of detailed concreteness with abstract precision, its exploration of common experiences and its elucidation of common sense, and, above all, the intelligibility, reasonableness, and fairness of its exposition of free choice not only in the context of opposing views but also in the context of all relevant psychological, ethical, and metaphysical considerations—the meaning of voluntariness and of responsibility, the role of passions, the promptings of desire and the aspirations of love, the pursuit of happiness, the limitations of reason, the aspirations of the will, and the several principles of causality in their relation to one another and as they operate in the realms of matter and spirit or in the singularly human conjunction of body and mind.[10]

In short, as Willis D. Nutting has put it: "You will find that you will understand any problem better if you can read something that Yves Simon has written on it. 'He touched nothing that he did not adorn.' "[11]

A SANSCULOTTE THOMIST

Yves René Marie Simon was born in Cherbourg, France, March 14, 1903, the third son and the youngest child of Auguste and Blanche Berthe (Porquet dela Féronnière) Simon. His father was technical director of Etablissements Simon Frères, Cherbourg, manufacturers of agricultural machinery. The enterprise was founded by Yves' grandfather, Laurent Simon, an ingenious mechanic who devised a number of machines including a very effective apple crusher. Laurent Simon, who started as a poor journeyman, was a Republican, and a family legend has it that he was among the young men who threw lumps of coal at the imperial carriage when Napoleon III visited Cherbourg in 1858. Not caring much for religion himself, Laurent nevertheless sent his children to Catholic schools where, as Yves' father later said, they received good education. Yves' mother also had Catholic teachers. Orphaned at the age of thirteen, she was educated by the sisters of the Christian Schools of the Mercy at Tourlaville, not far from Cherbourg. Thus when the two of them married in 1894, they became a typical French Catholic conservative bourgeois family. But Yves R. Simon did not turn out as its typical product.

It was a happy family life, Yves recalled in a brief autobiographical sketch he wrote soon after coming to the United States, until both his brothers contracted tuberculosis in 1909. The eldest, René Laurent Marie, who studied law in Paris, died soon afterwards, while the other brother, Jean Albert Marie, spent years at sanitariums away from the family. Jean eventually recovered but, accepted as a volunteer in the army, was killed on the front in 1917. Yves himself did not escape misfortune. The illness that put him at the age of nine in a cast for several years left him lame for the rest of his life. But it did not damage either his mind or his spirit.

Looking back, Simon judged himself a rather mediocre student until the age of twelve when his last tutor, who happened to be an old teacher of the Lycée de Cherbourg, inspired in him genuine interest in learning and prepared him for the Latin and Greek section of the baccalaureate. By the fall of 1918, Yves had recovered enough to be able to attend regular classes, and in the next two years he passed "quite successfully" both parts of the curriculum. This program did not stress natural sciences, or history, or geography, but Simon enjoyed its main subject, philosophy. "I used then to write poetry," he recalled, "and I believed in my vocation as a poet with some sort of sincerity."[12] Planning eventually to enroll at the Ecole Normale Superieure, Yves at the age of seventeen went to Paris to attend classes at the Lycée Louis le Grand, where he signed up for a program called *rhetorique superieure*. This included the Latin, Greek, and French literature, ancient, medieval, and modern history, as well as some philosophy. He learned a great deal in this program and enjoyed the company of some outstanding fellow students,[13] but at the end of the year he decided that he would rather study philosophy as a regular university student. Thus in 1921 he enrolled simultaneously at the Sorbonne and at the Catholic University of Paris, earning in the next two years both *license-en-philosophie* at Sorbonne, and the *Diplome d'E-tudes Superieures de Philosophie* at the Catholic University. At that time, Jacques Maritain was on the faculty of the Catholic University, and

Simon was greatly impressed both by the man and by his teaching. At Sorbonne, where the courses offered were not integrated, Simon at least learned about working methods in various fields of research. What Maritain taught, however, persuaded Simon that rather than "as a mere cultural exercise," philosophy must be taken seriously as search for truth and wisdom.[14]

Nevertheless, it took Simon several years before he finally made up his mind about what he wanted to do. Immediately upon graduation, he took a clerical job at the Ministry of Education, conveniently located near the National Library. At the Sorbonne, he had been introduced to the great French social thinkers of the nineteenth century, and so he spent much of his free time reading the works of Saint-Simon and various Saint-Simonists, plus Fourier, Considerant, and Buchez. But when he discovered "the greatest social thinker of the period, P.-J. Proudhon," he dropped the others. "Indefatigably," he reports, he read and re-read the forty odd volumes of the works of Proudhon and "studied his biography, character and influence in great detail."[15]

Simon was not persuaded by Proudhon's anarchism, but he was impressed by Proudhon's deep sense for social justice. As Simon read him, Proudhon was not entirely wrong in his criticism of wealth and property and was definitely right in upholding the dignity of the individual, especially the worker. Moreover, what Proudhon was arguing in his rather rambling essays on these matters was not, in Simon's view, all that different from what Aquinas taught in his tightly organized scholastic mode. For instance, both of them relegate the pursuit of material wealth to a low priority among human pursuits. And as he was thus combining the insights of a nineteenth-century anarchist and a thirteenth-century saint in his own mind, Simon on at least one occasion referred to himself as "a sansculotte Thomist."[16] The best-known French Thomists of that time were no more sympathetic to the revolutionary republican ideal than were the members of the influential *Action Française*, many of whom yearned for the restoration of monarchy. By contrast, Simon was committed to *liberté, eqalité, fraternité*, to *La Republique*, and to democracy. Studying Proudhon-cum-Aquinas may thus be said to have had something to do with his deep conviction that the search for truth is inseparable from the pursuit of liberty, equality, and social justice.

These social feelings as well as his personal experience with illness led Simon, in 1926, to enroll in medical school, where as a conscientious, hard-working student he learned a great deal about anatomy, physiology, and chemistry, as well as about scientific methodology. But in 1928, he decided that philosophy rather than medicine is his calling, and he reenrolled at the Catholic University. He concentrated on Scholastic philosophy and studied "exhaustively" the basic works of Aristotle and of St. Thomas and his commentators. In a year, he earned the degree of *Lector Philosophie*, and began work on his proposed dissertation on the ontology of knowledge. Waiting for a suitable position at some university, he studied German and spent some time in Breslau. He also kept busy newly translating some Latin texts of St. Thomas and contributing articles on a variety of philosophical subjects to the *Revue de Philosophie* and *La Vie Intellectuelle*. Finally, in 1930, he received his first academic appointment. He became professor of philosophy at the Catholic University of Lille. In the same year, he married Paule Louise Dromard, and they settled in a busy domestic and academic life.

Simon became the managing editor of the *Revue de Philosophie* and general editor of two book series, "Cours et Documents de Philosophie" and "Le Beaux Voyages d'Autrefois," published by Pierre Téqui in Paris. He also became involved in politics, and in 1934 Simon wrote a statement "Pour le bien commun" for a manifesto on "Les Reponsibilités du Chrétien et le Moment Présent," signed by fifty other prominent citizens reacting to the horrors of the Spanish civil war. By then, he had finished his dissertation on the ontology of knowledge, and he published it along a companion volume on moral knowledge. He continued to write scholarly articles on Christian philosophy, the philosophy of science, and the philosophy of nature, but became increasingly interested also in social problems. Thus in 1936, in addition to his political tract on the Ethiopian war, mentioned above, he translated, for a collection edited by Jacques Maritain called "La Lumiere Ouvrière," *Das gewerbliche Proletariat*, by Goetz A. Briefs.[17] He was himself keenly interested in the subject of work, and workers, and two years later he published three monographs on the definition of work, the relation between work and wealth, and the prospects for a "culture ouvrière."[18] By that time his reputation, at least in Catholic circles, had crossed the borders of France, and in 1938, upon recommendation by Waldemar Gurian and Etienne Gilson, Simon was invited to come to the United States as a Visiting Professor of Philosophy at the University of Notre Dame.

The outbreak of the Second World War prevented Simon's return to France, and as it happened, he never went back even for a visit. Adjusting quickly to the new academic environment, Simon gave a paper on "Liberty and Authority" at the annual meeting of the American Catholic Philosophical Association in 1939, and in 1940, he was invited to give the annual Aquinas Lecture for the Aristotelian Society at Marquette University.[19] In the same year, he also published versions of his essays on work and wealth in his own English translation in *The Review of Politics*.[20] As the war in Europe escalated, however, Simon turned to more political writing. In addition to the books mentioned above, he wrote articles mostly for the *Commonweal* and *La Nouvelle Relève* (Montreal). He also helped refugees from Nazism come to the United States, and he went on lecturing tours in the United States, Canada, and Mexico. In 1943, he was awarded an honorary degree by the University of Mexico. By then, of course, the United States had also entered the war, and a certain tension he had felt in the early years at Notre Dame was greatly reduced. It is now seldom remembered, but the Catholic hierarchy in America had not only supported the Francoist party in the Spanish civil war but had also carefully refrained from criticizing the Pètain regime in occupied France. The only Catholic organization that took an antifascist stand was the group associated with Dorothy Day and *The Catholic Worker*, and even though he rejected their radical pacifism, Simon found occasional contact with them refreshing.

Simon was adamant about the need to destroy the evil of fascism. Thus out of a mixture of anger, sadness, and hope, he wrote a letter to his friend Edmond Michelet on June 12, 1940, in which he prophesized that "the Nazis will not win this war; it will be won by the United States, but God only knows at what price in suffering for our country."[21] While today this reads as a statement of fact, this was written six days before the famous appeal by Charles de Gaulle to the French to continue fighting and a full eighteen months before the Japanese attack on Pearl Harbor. At the same time, Simon apparently experienced also a unique personal development, which is wonderfully described in a remembrance by another of his old French friends. What most impressed Paul Vigneau when he met Simon in 1942 was "la remarquable unité personnelle d'un professeur français devenant Américain, métaphysicien et moraliste, à la fois mâitre en thomisme et en civisme: celui-ci évidemment nourri d'un enthusiasme démocratique inspiré de l'ideologie des États-Unis et de leur expérience."[22]

Indeed, after the war, several of his friends in France urged Simon to write a book on the contemporary American civilization. He was flattered by their thinking him qualified, but the enormity of the task, he pleaded, would require the abilities of a "historical and sociological genius" even greater than Tocqueville. Nevertheless, recognizing how important American experience was for the rest of the world, Simon asked his colleagues at Notre Dame to submit essays in their fields of expertise, which he would then translate for the French readers and for which he would provide an appropriate Introduction. The result was a collection entitled *La Civilisation Américaine*, published in Paris in 1950, and translated into Italian in 1953.[23] The essays by various authors report on labor, rural life, family, race relations, economic system, domestic and foreign policies, education, religion, and literature. Today, these reports are mostly of historical interest, as they reveal how much the country has changed in the last half century. And this is, uncharacteristically, true also of some of Simon's comments in the Introduction. For instance, while he denounced discrimination against African-Americans as an unacceptable antinomy at the heart of the American way of life, Simon wrote as if he expected the problem to be worked out in the not too distant future. With hindsight, we know that his timing was wrong. Simon was also wrong in his optimistic comments on the prospects of the labor movement, whose strength and influence, as it turned out, have since declined considerably in the American political and social life. But if not as prediction, one can still appreciate his comments as a constructive proposal with regard to potential contribution that a decently organized labor could make to the development of democratic society. Finally, however, some questions Simon raised about the then prevailing pragmatic-progressive type of education seem to attract attention once again. Stressing adaptation to social environment as if that was the same as adaptation to physical environment, did not seem to Simon the best way to educate free and responsible democratic citizens. Today's calls for "return to the basics" as well as for "value education" may not be exactly what Simon would endorse without qualification, but they do confirm the point of his criticism. Democracy needs education in basic values.

AT THE UNIVERSITY OF CHICAGO

Simon left the University of Notre Dame in 1948 to join the Committee on Social Thought at the University of Chicago, and he remained on its faculty until his death in 1961. The membership of this graduate committee, which has an open interdisciplinary program and grants its own doctoral degrees, included then in addition to John U. Nef, an economic historian who was its founder and longtime chair, also Friedrich A. Hayek and Frank Knight (Economics), Edward A. Shills (Sociology), David Green (Classics), Peter H. von Blankenhagen (Archeology), Otto von Simpson (Art History), and Mircea Eliade (Comparative Religion). For his debut, as it were, Simon presented the annual Charles A. Walgreen Foundation Lectures, which were published in 1951 under the title, *Philosophy of Democratic Government*. The book was translated into Japanese and Portuguese in 1955, into German in 1956, and into Korean in 1960. Since then it has also been translated into Italian in 1983, and most recently into Polish in 1993. The original English volume continued to be reprinted in various editions by the University of Chicago Press for more than thirty years, and, with a detailed new index, it is now available from the University of Notre Dame Press.

Simon's *Philosophy of Democratic Government* is a comprehensive historical-theoretical treatise on the nature and the potential as well as the limitations of democracy that has stood well the test of time. In fact, one may say that the collapse of communism and the developments in the so-called Third World now taking place in the midst of deep postmodern perplexities make Simon's interpretation of democracy even more relevant today than when he first offered it in the afterglow of the victory over fascism. Today, the spread of global capitalism often enough thwarts people's democratic aspirations, and the prevailing schools of philosophy and social sciences do not help much either. To appreciate fully Simon's intellectual commitment to democracy, however, his political theory needs to be aligned with the rest of his philosophical achievement.

Interested in making available in English some classic texts in the Thomistic tradition, Simon with two collaborators invested eight years in translating a part of the treatise on logic by John Poinsot (1589–1644), also known as John of Saint Thomas. While this is a hefty tome of over six hundred pages, the main reason why it took him and his team so long to do the translation was that they were determined not to send the manuscript to the printer until they had succeeded in rendering every technical term of the ancient Latin text into readable, idiomatic English. But what to some may thus appear an esoteric academic enterprise had for its authors also a sound practical purpose. They wanted to show that "material logic" rather than an outdated and useless scholastic exercise remains a viable intellectual tool of many uses. As Simon explains in the Foreword, while "no part or function of logic will ever decide whether a particular proposition, relative to the real world is true," properly conducted material logic is quite capable of telling us "what general conditions an argumentation must satisfy in order to be not only consistent, i.e., formally perfect, but also demonstrative."[24] As we shall see in the chapters that follow, Simon pays scrupulous attention to these demonstrative conditions in all his investigations.

Logic, however, is by no means the only topic whose mastery strengthens Simon's defense of democracy as "the best regime." In his eleven years as a regular teaching member of the Committee on Social Thought, Simon offered twenty-seven courses covering roughly the same number of distinct subjects. The list is as follows: Freedom of Choice and the Ethics of Liberty; The Object of Aristotelian Logic; General Metaphysics of Knowledge; Nature of Practical Wisdom; Causality and Contingency; Definition of Philosophy; Pre-Marxian Socialism; Non-Marxian Socialism; Proudhon; Introduction to Metaphysics; On Motion, Place and Time; On Unity and Plurality in the Physical Universe; The Problem of Life; The Problem of Memory; From Experience to Understanding; Liberty and Community; Political Government; General Theory of Authority; The Theory of Being; The Metaphysics of Love; Theoretical Philosophy in Its Relation to the Sciences; Foundations of Ethics; Theory of Virtues; The Problem of Natural Law; On Work and the Workman; Nature and Forms of Analogy; and last but not least, The Critique of Scientific Knowledge. Clearly, offering courses on such a variety of topics is not the usual practice among academicians. But Simon did it for a specific purpose. He was planning a "Philosophical Encyclopedia" of many volumes, which was to include most subjects in metaphysics, epistemology, moral and political philosophy, philosophy of science, and logic, as well as such hard to classify topics as work and culture. And although this may look like a plan for a one-man revival of learning, few of those who knew Simon would consider it to have been beyond his reach. Indeed, had he not died at the age of fifty-eight, Simon could have given us a spectacular contemporary example of what feats the human mind is really capable of, especially when the man puts his heart into it as well.[25]

When Simon learned that his illness was terminal, he renamed his project "Philosophical Inquiries," in which he planned to cover only certain key topics from the proposed "Encyclopedia." His time, however, was running out, and he died leaving his work unfinished.[26] Still, not everything was lost. Based on the manuscripts and notes he had left behind, his friends, former students, and others attracted to his work have been able to bring out nine posthumous books so far. Additional volumes are in preparation. And even though these publications by different editors may not be a match for a *summa* that was never to be, they nevertheless represent an impressive *corpus* and reconfirm Simon's reputation as a Master Teacher.

But what exactly did Simon teach, and what exactly can one learn from him? A campus joke in his time went like this: The University of Chicago is a Baptist institution where Jewish professors teach Catholic doctrine to atheistic students. Did Simon teach Catholic doctrine? Reviewers of his books to this day routinely inform the readers that Simon worked in the Aristotelian-Thomistic philosophic tradition, and sometimes they identify him as "a Catholic philosopher." Both these denominations are correct, and Simon certainly would be the last to reject them. But as information, this needs to be elaborated. For one thing, historical Thomism is by no means a unified or even a coherent school of philosophy. For example, leaving aside earlier conflicts over the centuries, the most recent distinctions that would have to be made in "Neo-Thomism" are between "transcendental" Thomism, "existential" Thomism, and "personalist" Thomism, each of which moreover is expounded in several variations. To mention only a few of the better known names, Étienne Gilson, Joseph Pieper, Bernard Lonergan, Gabriel Marcel, Jacques Maritain, Louis de Raeymaeker, Reginald Gerrigou-Lagrange, Ferdinand van Steenberghen, and Henry de Lubac are all listed as Thomists, but they divide on many issues among themselves. In fact, one book currently popular among Thomists bears the title, *From Unity to Pluralism: The Internal Evolution of Thomism.*[27] And at a 1992 meeting of the American Maritain Association, the author of that book raised additional questions in a paper entitled, "Is Thomas's Way of Philosophizing Still Viable Today?"[28]

In his interpretation of Aquinas, Simon is closest to Maritain, but they by no means agree on every issue.[29] Thus in order to evaluate Simon's philosophical work objectively, it helps to recall the opinion of the reviewer of his doctoral dissertation. "The author follows Saint Thomas and his commentators," the reviewer noted, "but he has assimilated the Thomist doctrine so perfectly, and he expounds it in a manner so personal that, were it not for the references, one could hardly guess the origin of his theories. Quite often it comes as a surprise to realize that certain of his points dealing with very modern issues rest on faithful interpretations of passages from Thomas Aquinas, from Cajetan, or from John of St. Thomas."[30] What Simon is interested in are not "texts" but actual problems, and he finds the Aristotelian-Thomistic tradition helpful in suggesting solutions. He may thus be considered a follower of that tradition because he succeeded, in a relatively short working life, to clarify, bring up to date, and even improve its teaching on a number of vital philosophical issues. And his originality is perhaps best appreciated precisely in the context of the twentieth-century political thought. Simon celebrates the ideals of liberty, equality, civil rights, and social justice drawing upon a tradition that had never before been associated with democracy.[31]

There are, of course, both Thomists and non-Thomists who would deny that the Thomist philosophy can ever be truly reconciled with democratic ideals. Simon was not unaware of this problem and did his best to clarify his position soon after he arrived in the United States. A discussion of Thomism and democracy, he wrote, may proceed in the manner of a historical investigation, and its task then would be to disentangle from many texts scattered in the work of St. Thomas what he actually thought about democratic regimes he knew about. But, Simon suggested, it should also be possible to work out a Thomistic approach to the problems of democracy as they appear to us. That was what he was interested in, and as he studied the thought of the "Angelic Doctor," he concluded that the concepts of the common good, authority, autonomy, freedom, and equality, among others, elaborated within the realist Thomist treatment of human nature, society, and politics, could much benefit our own understanding of democratic theory and practice. Indeed, it was Aquinas' "sublime theory of liberty, developed with great thoroughness and unmatched accuracy," not in his political writings but in his psychological, metaphysical, and theological treatises—where few had looked for it—which convinced Simon that rather than just being able to support democratic ideals, Thomism may be said to require them. He wrote:

Whoever has understood the ideas of St. Thomas on liberty as a mastery enjoyed by rational beings, on the grounds of their rational nature itself, over the means that lead to their ends; whoever has understood the meaning of the Thomistic thesis that liberty is an attribute of the divine nature, a divine name, should conclude that the general philosophy of St. Thomas involves a philosophy of political liberty that is both very orderly and very radical.[32]

Whether this interpretation of political liberty that not only justifies democracy in theory but calls for its establishment in practice can or should, when actually developed, still be called Thomist is a moot point. For instance, in a lengthy review of Simon's *Philosophy of Democratic Government*, Leo Strauss argues that the philosophy of Thomas Aquinas can never be divorced from its "conservative" context and placed in service to democracy. After all, Strauss points out, none of its greatest exponents ever discovered its democratic potential alleged by Simon.[33] But that may well be to Simon's credit. Although he refers to and quotes Aquinas, and Aristotle, often enough, Simon does not rest his arguments on their authority. In his demonstrations, Simon appeals to our reasoning powers and, with reference to political and moral issues, to common sense and experience. The degree of allegiance to a particular school of philosophy, then, is perhaps not the best way to judge Simon's interpretation of democracy. It makes more sense to consider his contribution as his own. Reviewing Simon's political theory along those of Raymond Aron and Bertrand de Jouvenel, Maurice Cranston does so. Simon's early death, he writes, "has deprived the Western world of one of its most original and distinguished political theorists."[34]

With regard to his being classified as a "Catholic philosopher," the truth of the matter is that Simon did his best to keep his religion and his philosophical work separate from each other. In a tribute to Jacques Maritain, which happened to had been his very last public lecture, Simon distinguished his own approach from that of his teacher and friend as follows. Maritain, Simon noted, did not always treat philosophical problems in strict isolation from religion. Maritain did that, Simon explained, because he saw the issues involved "related vitally, though not essentially, in the longings of people for the truths that matter most in terms of human destiny." Though he could have chosen differently, "if he had his own way," Simon suggested, Maritain had to follow his "calling as a Christian philosopher" and will be so recognized in history. As for himself, Simon confessed preference for "the method of isolation." Keeping philosophy and theology separate, he said, "furnishes special guarantees of epistemological purity and logical rigor." And, Simon added, this appears to be the method recommended by Aquinas himself.[35]

THE PHILOSOPHER'S CALLING

Simon readily acknowledges that no philosopher can escape completely the influence of his time, social environment, or his own background and personality. Philosophers, after all, are human, and all philosophies include an inevitable admixture of ideology, expressing the aspirations of a given society at a given point in its history.[36] Nevertheless, some philosophers and their philosophies are less ideological than others, as may be seen by comparing the teachings of, say, Spinoza, John Locke, and Herbert Spencer.[37] But the influence of ideology is not the only problem that philosophers must face. While other sciences exist almost exclusively in a technically elaborate state, which strongly discourages lay involvement in scientific disputes, philosophy exists also in a popular state which admits all to its discussions. And consequently, interpretations by people without real understanding of the technical aspects of philosophical issues sometimes come to prevail socially.[38] In contrast to other scientists, then, the philosopher has to struggle against error on two fronts, so to speak, the popular as well as the professional. Discouraged by this prospect, some philosophers may be tempted to retreat to the relatively greater safety of academic debates, but not Simon. Rather than as a mere "cultural exercise," Simon takes philosophy seriously as the search for truth and wisdom, from which no one must be excluded. All human beings "by nature desire to know." But according to Simon, philosophers have another equally important reason not to withdraw from the popular debates of philosophical issues. The dedicated philosopher will want to remain involved with his community precisely because "all real freedom is contained within limits of the knowledge of truth."[39]

Amidst opinions prevailing today, both in the academy and on the street, this affirmation of the unity of truth and freedom is bound to be viewed with suspicion. Fashionable contemporary philosophies and mainstream social science have more or less convinced people that, if there were such a thing as truth, freedom would be impossible.[40] Some legal philosophers also try to save freedom from truth. As one famous judge puts it, the spirit of liberty "is not sure that it is right."[41] And according to another, "[t]he best test of truth is the power of thought to get itself accepted in the free competition of the market."[42] How the liberty "which is not sure that it is right" might fare in such competition is not clear, but most people who consider themselves philosophical and political liberals do not seem to worry too much about it. But Simon, for one, does not think that "uncertain liberty" is best for democracy.

Where, Simon asks, do we find the most unmistakable examples of the spirit of what we call liberty, freedom, free will, free choice? In uncertain, perplexed, weak-willed, anxious, and highly suggestible people? Or in persons in firm control of their images and emotions, who know what they know and what they do not know, who know what they want, and who, as Simon sees it, "at the summit of human energy hold that death itself is an accident which cannot affect their relation to the really important ends of human life?"[43] Liberty belongs to heroes and saints, he writes, and "the literary characters who seek mobility in order to avoid tough decisions" would have neither prestige nor imitators were it not that "the cultivation of passive indifference provides a cheap substitute of freedom to intellectuals who no longer have any sense of freedom."[44] Thus contrary to what some may think, it is Patrick Henry who had the spirit of liberty; Hamlet suffered from the lack of it.

All told, then, the philosopher's calling is a demanding one, because it requires more than just a good mind. For instance, "doing" philosophy primarily in order to be recognized as a learned person is a kind of cheating. But pursuing knowledge exclusively for its own sake, without regard to social recognition, is also wrong. One must want to know for the sake of truth, not for the pleasure of knowing. There is such a thing as intellectual gluttony and, like any other addiction, it takes away one's freedom. Thus the true "freedom of the intellect" requires the philosopher first to achieve "freedom from the self."[45] Jacques Maritain describes this necessary condition as follows:

> The act of philosophizing involves the character of the philosopher. Pride, envy, vanity, gluttony and intellectual avarice, the preference of dialectical virtuosity and the false security of academicism to the mys-

tery of being, the spirit of sectarianism and zealous bitterness, a taste for what is fashionable, self-satisfaction or satisfaction with a group or circle, the duplicity which turns against known truth, are all fatal to the rectitude of the philosophical act.[46]

According to Simon, in order to remain true to its calling, those who pursue philosophy must be ready to pass its ultimate test. To prove their committment to the objective pursuit of truth and wisdom, philosophers must be ready at any time "to suspend their philosophical pursuit to help a fellow in need of a job, an outlaw in need of a refuge, a soul in need of God." If a philosopher can do that, he or she has indeed attained freedom from the self and can then stand as a credible defender of the unity of freedom and truth. Simon does not hesitate to assert that "in order to remain love of truth," philosophy "must be totally subordinated to charity."[47] But by this he does not mean that strength of character is all one needs to investigate the mystery in which our knowledge of the world, life, history, and society remains forever wrapped. Like any other scientists, philosophers need tools appropriate to their discipline. Simon notes that many projects in search of "meaning" in our time brim with ideas and are pursued with earnest dedication. What he misses in most of them, however, is precisely "scientific rigor." For instead of things like "the tragic sentiment of life," "immersion in history," "experience of death," "esprit de finesse," "our cultural heritage," etc., what philosophical inquiry requires above all, Simon writes, is

clarity in the statement of questions and principles, firmness of inference, rational evidence of conclusions, appropriateness in predication, integral preservation of past development, lucid order, and the unique defense against error that rational forms alone can provide.[48]

In intellectual work, especially at its loftier levels, Simon points out, it is relatively easy to conceal error under the cover of erudition. A theory may be wrong, but if it shows intellectual ingenuity, it may still be praised as a magnificent piece of scholarship, and may well be also all its author is after. But as this is something that cannot happen in judging manual work, Simon suggests holding up the latter as a symbolic ideal for intellectual work. "The slightest defect in a key makes it impossible to unlock the door, and nobody can be fooled." Now to describe philosophy as the key to truth makes sense beyond metaphor, and letting "the most humble kinds of work" serve as a model for its culture and search for intellectual perfection may well be of special benefit to democratic society. The lover of truth and the manual worker, Simon holds, have much in common.[49]

Simon recognizes that the life of the philosopher is not for everyone. The work is difficult, success is not guaranteed, and not all citizens are fond of philosophers. Moreover, since philosophical work with its many trials and errors is done mostly in solitude, the philosopher cannot count on the comfort that teamwork often brings to other scientists. Yet for those who choose it and persist in it, the philosopher's life does have its own profoundly human reward. This reward comes, Simon writes, when the philosopher breaks out of his solitude and succeeds in communicating, together with a particle of truth, something of the aspirations, something of the dedication, something of the hope and love that keep him going through never-ending difficulties. And this is why "a philosopher who has ever succeeded in communicating his inspiration together with his demonstration, and who has experienced the joy of friendship born of such communication, will always feel that if he had to choose again, philosophy would again be his calling."[50]

NOTES

1. Yves R. Simon, *Introduction à l'ontologie du connaître* (Paris: Desclée de Brouwer, 1934); reprint, William C. Brown Reprint Library, Dubuque, IA, 1965; English translation by Vukan Kuic and Richard J. Thompson, *An Introduction to Metaphysics of Knowledge* (New York: Fordham University Press, 1990). *Critique de la connaissance morale* (Paris: Desclée de Brouwer, 1934).

2. Yves R. Simon, *La campagne d'Ethiopie et la pensée politique française* (Paris: Desclée de Brouwer, 1936).

3. *Book of Catholic Authors* (Grosse Pointe, MI: Walter Romig Publisher, 1945), p. 269.

4. Yves R. Simon, *La grande crise de la République Française: Observations sur la vie politique français de 1918 à 1938* (Montreal: Éditions de l'Arbre, 1941); English translation, *The Road to Vichy* (New York: Sheed and Ward, 1942); reprinted by University Press of America, Lanham, MD, 1988.

5. Yves R. Simon, *La Marche à la délivrance* (New York: Éditions de la Mai-

son Française, 1942); English translation, *The March to Liberation* (Milwaukee, WI: Tower Press, 1942).

6. Yves R. Simon, *Par delà l'expérience du désespoir* (Montreal: Lucien Parizeau, 1945); English translation by Willard R. Trask, *The Community of the Free* (New York: Henry Holt, 1947); reprinted by University Press of America, Lanham, MD, 1984.

7. Robert Speath in *The Review of Politics*, vol. 48, no. 1, Winter 1986, pp. 121–22.

8. Review of Yves R. Simon, *Work, Society, and Culture*, ed. Vukan Kuic (New York: Fordham University Press, 1971, 1987), in *Annals of the American Academy*, vol. 411 (1974), p. 229.

9. Louis de Raeymaeker, *Revue Neoscholastique de Philosophie* (Louvain), vol. 38 (1935), pp. 509–11.

10. Yves R. Simon, *Freedom of Choice*, ed. Peter Wolf (New York: Fordham University Press, 1969, 1987), pp. xi–xii.

11. Review of *Work, Society, and Culture* in *The Review of Politics*, vol. 34, no. 1, Winter 1972, p. 239.

12. *Book of Catholic Authors*, p. 263.

13. Among them Paul Vignaux, who later became Dean at the Ecole Normale Supérieure, and Eduard Michelet, who held several ministerial positions during the Presidency of Charles de Gaulle. Simon remained in touch with both of them in later years.

14. Simon, "Mes premiers souveniers de Jacques Maritain," *New Scholasticism*, vol. 56, no. 2 (1982), pp. 200–206.

15. See Simon, "Le problème de la transcendence et le défi de Proudhon," *Nova et Vetera* (Geneva) 9 (1934): 225–38; English translation by Charles P. O'Donnell and Vukan Kuic in *Thought*, vol. 54, no. 1 (1979), pp. 177–85; also "Notes sur le fédéralisme proudhonnien," *Esprit*, April 1937, no. 5, pp. 53–65; English translation by Vukan Kuic in *Publius*, vol. 3, no. 2 (1973), pp. 19–30. Simon had officially registered Proudhon as the topic for his doctoral dissertation at the Sorbonne in 1924 but did not follow through with it.

16. In a letter to Maritain, Simon wrote: "Remember, I am the only sansculotte who since 1922, has tied himself to you and your philosophy, despite your affinity for the *Action Française* and those horrible characters who would come to shake your hand at the end of your lectures at the Institute Catholique." See John Hellman, "Yves R. Simon, Maritain, and the Vichy Catholics," Introduction to *The Road to Vichy*, 1988 edition, p. viii.

17. Goetz A. Briefs, *Le prolétariat industriel*, trans. Yves R. Simon (Paris: Desclée de Brouwer, 1936).

18. Yves Simon, *Trois leçons sur le travail* (Paris: Pierre Téqui, 1938).

19. Proceedings of the American Catholic Philosophical Association (Wash-

ington, DC), vol. 16 (1940), pp. 86–114; reprinted in Yves R. Simon, *Freedom and Community*, ed. Charles P. O'Donnell (New York: Fordham University Press, 1968); Yves R. Simon, *Nature and Function of Authority* (Milwaukee, WI: Marquette University Press, 1940).

20. Simon, "Work and Workman," *The Review of Politics*, vol. 2, no. 1, Winter 1940, pp. 63–86; "Work and Wealth," *The Review of Politics*, vol. 2, no. 2, Spring 1940, pp. 197–217.

21. Edmond Michelet, "Mon Ami Yves Simon," *Nova et Vetera* (Geneva), vol. 43, no. 3, June–September 1966, pp. 208–13.

22. Paul Vignaux, "Yves Simon: Par dela l'expérience du désespoir," *Revue Philosophique de Louvain*, vol. 70, no. 2, May 1972, pp. 237–39.

23. Yves R. Simon, ed., *La Civilisation Américaine* (Paris: Desclée de Brouwer, 1950); *Civiltà americana* (Milan: Vita e Pensiero, 1953).

24. *The Material Logic of John of St. Thomas*, tr. Yves R. Simon, John J. Glanville, and G. Donald Hollenhorst (Chicago: University of Chicago Press, 1955), p. xi.

25. Some years after Simon's death, John Nef, the founder and longtime chairman of the Committee on Social Thought, recalled how Simon was invited to join them because he so clearly shared their "belief in the reality of truth, in the realm of being, and in man's capacity, by research in philosophy, to edge a little closer to it." In his actual performance in the Committee, Nef added, Simon far surpassed all their expectations. "John U. Nef Recalls Yves Simon," *University of Chicago Magazine*, vol. 64, no. 5, May–June 1972, pp. 37–38.

26. See Paule Simon, "The Papers of Yves R. Simon," *The New Scholasticism*, vol. 32, no. 4, Fall 1963, pp. 501–507.

27. Gerald A. McCool, S.J., *From Unity to Pluralism: The Internal Evolution of Thomism* (New York: Fordham University Press, 1988).

28. Gerald A. McCool, "Is Thomas's Way of Philosophizing Still Viable Today?" in *The Future of Thomism*, ed. Deal W. Hudson and Dennis Wm. Moran (American Maritain Association, 1992), pp. 51–64. The collection of papers in this volume is a good introduction to today's varieties of "Thomism." The book is distributed by the University of Notre Dame Press.

29. For instance, Simon believes the distinction between "civilization" and "culture" to be much more important than suggested by Maritain. See *Work, Society, and Culture*, pp. 155–56. Likewise, contrary to what he takes to be Maritain's position, Simon firmly believes that aesthetic judgments can be objective. See *Moral Virtue*, pp. 83–84, 89.

30. Raeymaeker *Revue Neoscholastique*, vol. 38 (1935), p. 509.

31. See John P. Hittinger, "Jacques Maritain and Yves R. Simon's Use of Thomas Aquinas in Their Defense of Liberal Democracy," in *Thomas Aquinas and His Legacy*, ed. David M. Gallagher, Studies in Philosophy and the History

of Philosophy, vol. 28 (Washington, DC: Catholic University of America Press, 1994), 149–72.

32. Yves R. Simon, "Thomism and Democracy," in *Science, Philosophy, and Religion: Second Symposium,* by Louis Finkelstein and Lyman Bryson (New York: The Conference on Science, Philosophy and Religion in Their Relations to the Democratic Way of Life, Inc., 1942), vol. 2, pp. 258–72.

33. See Leo Strauss, *What is Political Philosophy?* (Westport, CT: Greenwood Press, 1959), pp. 306–11; the review was originally published in *The New Scholasticism,* July 1952.

34. Maurice Cranston, "Political Philosophy in Our Time," in *The Great Ideas Today* (Chicago: Encyclopedia Britannica, 1975), p. 126.

35. Yves R. Simon, "Jacques Maritain: The Growth of a Christian Philosopher," in *Jacques Maritain: The Man and His Achievement,* ed. Joseph W. Evans (New York: Sheed and Ward, 1963), pp. 3–24.

36. Yves R. Simon, *The Tradition of Natural Law,* ed. Vukan Kuic (New York: Fordham University Press, 1965, 1992), pp. 16–20.

37. *Work, Society, and Culture,* p. 108.

38. Simon, "The Community of Intellects," *Cap and Gown* (Notre Dame, IN: University of Notre Dame Press, December 1957), pp. 5–6.

39. *The Community of the Free,* p. 4.

40. Yet Simon suspects that there must be more than just a few social scientists who, "intuitively, emotionally, and morally dedicated to liberty, wish at the bottom of their hearts that social science should always be so imperfect as to leave plenty of room for trials and errors and for the arbitrariness of individual preference." *Freedom of Choice,* pp. 157–58.

41. See Learned Hand, *The Spirit of Liberty,* ed. I. Dillard (New York: Knopf, 1952), p. 190.

42. The market test for truth was suggested by Justice Oliver Wendell Holmes in his dissent in *Abrams vs. United States* (250 U.S. 616, 1919). Simon quotes the line in *A General Theory of Authority* (Notre Dame, IN: University of Notre Dame Press, 1962, 1980), p. 115.

43. *Freedom of Choice,* p. 158.

44. *Freedom of Choice,* p. 122.

45. *Community of the Free,* pp. 120–23.

46. Jacques Maritain, *Science and Wisdom* (London: Geoffrey Bles, 1940), p. 146.

47. See *U.S. Catholic,* May 1968, pp. 43–44. Simon spoke on the occasion of the presentation to Maritain of an award for outstanding work in Christian Social Education by the Sheil School of Social Studies in Chicago on November 28, 1948.

48. *Material Logic,* p. xxiii.

49. Yves R. Simon, "The Concept of Work," in *The Works of the Mind*, ed. Robert B. Heywood (Chicago: University of Chicago Press, 1947, 1966), 16–17.

50. See Simon, "The Philosopher's Calling," *Proceedings of the American Catholic Philosophical Association* (Washington, DC), vol. 32 (1958), p. 31; reprinted in *A Philosopher at Work*, ed. Anthony O. Simon (Lanham, MD: Rowman and Littlefield, 1999).

2

PHILOSOPHY, SCIENCE, AND PRACTICAL WISDOM

I n the same year in which appeared Simon's *Philosophy of Democratic Government*, Hans Reichenbach published *The Rise of Scientific Philosophy*. With a strong background in mathematics, symbolic logic, and physics, Reichenbach reported that "a new philosophy had arisen from the grounds of science" and had indeed "proceeded from speculation to science." Past philosophical efforts, he wrote, were mostly wasted on environmentally induced "moral directives," which "by their nature cannot be true." For example, born in a poor middle-class family, his father a carpenter, his mother an ardent pietist, should one wonder that Kant was only too "happy and proud to derive in learned books the very morality he was imbued with in his nursery"?[1] Curiously enough, Reichenbach admitted that he, too, was the product of his environment, a staunch supporter of democracy, having been "imbued with its essence" since birth. As a philosopher, however, he felt obliged to do one better not only to Galileo [*Eppur si muove*] but also to Descartes [*Cogito ergo sum*]. "The correct analysis of the situation," that is, the strictly scientific philosophical answer to the question as to whether there is a world out there and how much we can know about it, Reichenbach wrote, is that "we have no absolutely conclusive evidence that there is a physical world and we have no absolutely conclusive evidence either that we exist."[2] Reichenbach did hasten to add that scientific philosophy had reasons to "posit" these existences. But he did not explain how these posits may relate to his "imbued" democratic beliefs.

Twenty years later, however, B. F. Skinner, taking up a much tougher stand in the name of science, denounced all political beliefs as vain illusions and urged that they be discarded once and for all as a first step toward a better future for all mankind. His book *Beyond Freedom and Dignity* did not please everyone, but there were those who praised its "scientific approach."[3] Skinner had earned his reputation by designing a method of "operant conditioning," in which instead of being punished for undesirable behavior subjects were rewarded for desirable behavior, and he had some success transferring this method from pigeons to humans. But Skinner's basic position is perhaps best conveyed with reference to a lecture he gave before a receptive audience, "On 'Having' a Poem." Lecturing, just like poetic composition, Skinner insisted, was the same thing as a goose laying an egg.[4] He made no reference in this lecture to political campaigns, debates, or voting.

Highlighted by these extreme examples are two confused and confusing trends prominent in the intellectual life of the past several generations. These trends are represented by a philosophy inspired by natural sciences that ends with reservations about external reality, and by a social science of the same inspiration that denies human freedom. This is an intriguing development, because the principles of liberty, equality, and the consent of the governed were the pride of the historical enlightenment that ushered modern science and philosophy. But history continues to move in mysterious ways, and the philosophical reservations about reality and scientific denials of freedom have not prevented democracy from becoming the world's preferred regime. Looking ahead, however, one is entitled to wonder how long the faith in democracy can be sustained in isolation from science and philosophy.

There is no simple explanation for this paradoxical situation. Most social scientists who do not believe in freedom and idealist philosophers who doubt the reality of the world apparently have no qualms about participating in the political life of their communities. But matters get more complicated when we discover that not every philosophical affirmation of the reality of the world and of human freedom provides equal support for meaningful democratic theory and practice. For instance, in *The Construction of Social Reality*, John R. Searle insists that "we live in one world, not two or three or seventeen" and that "realism and a correspondence conception [of truth] are essential presuppositions of any sane philosophy, not to mention science."[5] Searle acknowledges that "realism" has been interpreted in many ways in the history of philosophy, but he wants to defend its simplest, ontological meaning. There is, he holds, an external reality independent of whatever representations of it we may devise, and it is in this real world that we construct our own social reality. Searle is critical of "thinkers as diverse as Michael Dummet, Nelson Goodman, Thomas Kuhn, Paul Feyerabend, Hilary Putnam, Richard Rorty, Jacques Derrida, Humberto Maturana, Francesco Varela, and Terry Winograd," precisely because they all want to qualify and dilute this basic meaning of realism. They all take leave from "normal understanding."[6] To say that "the statements are true if and only if they correspond to the facts," is for Searle the only correct way to describe "the situation we are actually in with our use of the words 'true,' 'statement,' and 'fact.' "[7]

Searle nowhere mentions democracy in this book, but based on a concept he calls "the Background," and which includes all sorts of objective human "capacities," his theory of the construction of social reality clearly provides for government from reflection and choice. Social reality, e.g., property, marriage, government, Searle explains, is created by us, literally. "From dollar bills to cathedrals . . . we are constantly encountering new social facts where the facts exceed the physical features of the underlying physical reality."[8] As Searle goes on, however, his distinction between social and physical realities becomes increasingly uncertain. "Culture," he writes, "is the form that biology takes." Where others may see a sharp break between biology and culture, Searle stresses continuity. Judging, consciously and intentionally, Proust to be a better novelist than Balzac, he writes, is an integral part of "the chemistry of neurotransmitters such as serotonin and norepinephrine." In fact, the ultimate connection/distinction between physical and social realities, Searle explains, is found in our "biological capacity to make something symbolize—or mean, or express—something beyond itself." While this still makes some sense—we have to be alive to express ourselves— Searle's final example leaves one wondering. He concludes his exposition of the construction of social reality by asserting that in the last analysis what distinguishes the collective behavior of lions attacking a hyena and the Supreme Court making a constitutional decision is nothing but the "symbolism" of the latter.[9] It is not only that the example itself seems somehow unsuitable. What makes one wonder about Searle's brand of "realism" is his pairing it with "symbolism." Both the faith and the practice of democracy could well use a more realistic philosophical support.

And that is precisely what Simon, working with an ontology and epistemology that acknowledge more than just a "symbolic" difference between physical and social realities, provides in his philosophy of democratic government. Compared to any number of contemporary philosophies, the Aristotelian-Thomist realism has the great advantage of having worked out sensible distinctions between sheer existence, thought, and action. But before sketching the framework upholding Simon's construction of democratic political reality, it may useful to round off this quick sampling of contemporary schools by taking a look also at the defense of democracy by some academic philosophers who do not consider themselves "realists."

For example, in affirmation of his democratic convictions, Richard Rorty proclaims "The Priority of Democracy to Philosophy," even as he has to do it in the name of his own special kind of philosophy.[10] Described sometimes as "neo-pragmatism" or "humanist pragmatism," Rorty's position, as one commentator puts it, represents a considerable interpretive challenge. Rorty draws freely "from analytic philosophy, existentialism, hermeneutic phenomenology, deconstruction and pragmatism, from Dewey, James, Wittgenstein, Heidegger, Sartre, Gadamer, Foucault, and Derrida."[11] Combining fragments from these sources with spirited criticism of traditional schools, Rorty has ventured to offer original interpretations on any number of subjects. But as he tells it himself, he has set himself free in his thinking by consciously rejecting the quest for "reality and justice held in a single vision" (Yeats).[12] He does not believe that there is any way "to reach outside our language-game to an account of the relations between the language-game and 'the world' as its 'content.' "[13] Worrying about what is really "out there" is a futile exercise; knowledge is not "a matter of getting reality right, but rather a matter of acquiring habits of actions for coping with reality."[14] Logical or not, this is Rorty's "philosophy democratized."[15] But interestingly enough, Rorty also believes that in democracy "accommodation and tolerance must stop short of a willingness to work within any vocabulary which one's interlocutor wants to use, to take seriously any topic which he puts forward for discussion."[16] Does this mean, then, that when philosophy is democratized, "coping with reality" may require critical or unpopular views to be ostracized?

John Rawls has a different solution. To safeguard the integrity of liberal democracy, he wants its politics divorced from philosophy. "Philosophy in the search for truth about an independent metaphysical and moral order," he writes, "cannot provide a workable and shared basis for a political conception of justice in a democratic society."[17] Thus rather than upon general principles established "behind the veil of ignorance," as he once believed, justice in democratic society, Rawls now thinks, must be established by an "overlapping consensus" on specific political issues. But decreeing philosophy separate from democracy seems even less practical than putting it under democracy, and Rawls ends in an impasse the opposite of Rorty's. "The political good no matter how important," he still insists, "can never in general outweigh the transcendent values—certain religious, philosophical, and moral values—that may possibly come in conflict with it."[18] Does that mean, then, that on grounds of their personal beliefs, citizens are free to disregard democratic overlapping consensus?

The interesting question here is why do Rorty and Rawls feel the need to defend their democratic convictions in effect *against* "philosophy as an independent search for truth"? And the same question may be put to other authors quoted above. Deliberately or by default, they all either divide reality and justice into separate visions or let one cancel the other. Reichenbach praises democracy but doubts his own existence. Skinner insists that the somatic is the only reality. Searle turns politics into biological symbolism. Rorty dismisses reality and turns justice into a language game. And as we have just seen, Rawls wants to save both democracy and philosophy by divorcing them from each other.[19]

Now since most of these authors take democracy to be indeed the best regime, three possibilities suggest themselves. There may be something wrong with their philosophies; there may be something wrong with their conception of democracy; and one cannot exclude the possibility that both their conception of philosophy and their views of democracy leave something to be desired. Clearly, not all versions of realism, let alone Scientism, Idealism, or Pragmatism, can hold reality and justice in a single vision. But that is not a problem for Aristotelian-Thomist realism, which in Simon's hands provides a firm foundation for an orderly view of liberty, equality, and justice for all.[20]

TO BE, TO KNOW, TO ACT

Contrary to its historical reputation, and contrary also to the modern assumptions about the "unity of science," the defining feature of the

Aristotelian-Thomist philosophy is its *epistemological pluralism*. Thomist epistemology not only divides science into different kinds; it also recognizes a distinct knowledge that is indispensable for coping with reality. Now as noted in the preceding chapter, Thomism has been interpreted in different ways by different authors. For our purposes, however, it should suffice to condense its epistemology based on Jacques Maritain's classic, *The Degrees of Knowledge: Distinguish to Unite*.[21] As Maritain explains Aristotle's as well as Aquinas's teaching, knowing is best divided into three basic types, called, respectively, theoretical, practical, and productive. Addressing the question of what is and what it is, theoretical knowledge comprises natural sciences (physics), mathematics, and metaphysics. Practical knowledge, concerned with what is to be done, includes ethics, economics, and politics. And productive knowledge tells how to make things.

Leaving aside mathematics and metaphysics, and postponing the discussion of productive knowledge, *technology*, for later treatment, the basic difference between practical and theoretical knowledge may be roughly explained as follows. In contrast to the natural sciences (and mathematics and metaphysics), ethics, economics, and politics deal with things that can be otherwise than they are. The Aristotelian-Thomist philosophy does not equivocate either about the contingent nature of human experience or about the reality of choices available to us. In its realist approach, practical knowledge is not after "selfish genes," serotonin, territorial imperatives, invisible hands, or black boxes converting inputs into outputs. The question addressed by practical knowledge in all its three branches is not, What will happen? but rather, What to do? Practical knowledge is what we depend on to construct social reality and thereby, within certain natural limits, make a difference in our lives, individual and social. All practical knowledge aims at "the good for man," but as Aristotle explains, both ethics and economics depend ultimately on political acknowledgment of that good.[22]

In agreement with common sense, here it is well understood that the difference politics can make is contained within limits set by the nature of things as well as by human nature. Thus while people may prefer this or that type of regime, no society can do without politics altogether. Neither beasts nor gods, as Aristotle remarks, human beings are political animals destined by nature to some kind of organized life in common.

The latter condition is that which cannot be otherwise than it is, and as such is the subject not of practical but of theoretical knowledge.

But what does it mean to say that the object of theoretical, or strictly scientific, knowledge cannot be otherwise than it is? Given the ever new discoveries of modern science, this formulation may easily be misunderstood as yet another proof of the outdated dogmatism of the Aristotelian-Thomist philosophy. According to Thomas Kuhn, scientific knowledge progresses through revolutions, and when new paradigms replace the old, they show things to be rather different from what they "used to be."[23] Now Kuhn is, of course, correct as far as history of science is concerned. Ptolemaic world view is overthrown by Copernicus, and Einstein improves on Newton. But that history by no means invalidates the Aristotelian-Thomist definition of theoretical knowledge and of its object. As a realist school, Thomism assumes existence of things independent of our thought. But as far as the knowledge of these things is concerned, it is obvious that it cannot consist or be expressed except in demonstrated, proven propositions. Science, as Aristotle puts it, is "the scientifically known objects."[24]

Scientific knowledge in Aristotelian-Thomism is not supposed to be a mere saver of appearances. Its truth is said to be measured by its correspondence with facts, which, as John Searle says, is the only sane philosophy. Still, and precisely because of its thorough metaphysical realism, not to mention common sense, the definition of the object of theoretical knowledge as that which cannot be otherwise than it is must not be so inflated as to mean that any object of knowledge is absolutely identical with the thing of which it is knowledge. To know something for real does not mean to know it without a remainder. Our knowledge does not and cannot exhaust reality.[25] Thus if and when $E = mc^2$ is superseded by another fairly demonstrated physico-mathematical formula, the Aristotelian-Thomist definition of the object of theoretical knowledge will not have to be changed; it will apply equally to the new proposition. Kuhn stresses change in the evolution of science. But what any new Kuhnian normal science reasserts is precisely that, until the next "revolution," its paradigm cannot be otherwise than it is. And this is exactly how, contrary to some philosophers of science, most practicing scientists think of their science. They do not doubt that they are in touch with an external reality, but they will not be particularly surprised by even radical new scientific discoveries. For these scientists no less than for Aristotle and Aquinas, Maritain and Simon, or Searle, and contrary to Reichenbach, Rorty, and perhaps Rawls and Kuhn himself, science, that is, theoretical knowledge, is about what is. No one is saying that we can ever empty the world and its content of their mystery.[26]

We see, then, that contrary to widespread misunderstandings, the Aristotelian-Thomist epistemology recognizes both diversity in human knowledge and its progressive nature. As the title and the subtitle of Maritain's great treatise specify, before they can be organized into a unified system, various kinds of knowledge must be carefully distinguished from each other, precisely because they are different and address different problems. And as far as theoretical knowledge is concerned, according to Simon, the great advantage of the Thomist epistemology is that it provides a sound realistic alternative to the prevailing Cartesian-Kantian philosophy of science. Challenged by Hume's skepticism, Kant "saved" Newtonian physics by locating scientific principles that make sense of the content of the world in the human mind. Thus scientific knowledge, "with its characteristics of orderliness, determination, and universality is produced," according to Kant, "by the application of mental categories to the diversity of sense-experience data."[27] But Maritain's interpretation, according to Simon, liberates the science of phenomena from under this Kantian "idealist charter." The orderliness, determination, and universality of scientific knowledge in Thomist epistemology are not produced by our mind but are established rather by its carefully putting together the observable regularities in the behavior of things. And even though these regularities cannot reveal the "essence" of things (*das Ding an sich*), they not only describe things but also testify to their specific existence. For example, Simon writes, no one can tell what silver is in itself. But we can measure its specific weight, we know that it melts at 960.5 degrees, boils at 2000 degrees, etc., all of which makes it possible to distinguish it from any other chemical species. In Maritain's terminology, all that the *perinoetical* intellection of *empiriological* science does, or indeed can do, is to describe the phenomena. Yet this description, this "host of predicates," as Simon puts it, cannot "hail upon nothingness as its subject." Designated by the name silver, there is here present—though undisclosed—an ontological X which holds up the chemical definition, Ag. What Maritain has done, then, according to Simon, is to have succeeded, with the help of the Thomist realist epistemology, in explaining the science of nature in a way that owes nothing to the idealistic interpretation of the mind's activity.[28]

But the Thomist epistemology provides also a solid framework for an intelligent realistic theoretical interpretation of social experience that frees it from the reductionist/deterministic confusion in which modern social science has been trapped since its introduction in the late nineteenth century. And among Simon's philosophical achievements, using that framework to show that the intelligent choice in constructing a social reality best suited to fulfill man's rational and political nature is the choice of democracy, is not the least.

FROM SCIENCE OF NATURE TO SCIENCE OF SOCIETY

Most people would readily grant not only that the critique of scientific knowledge of nature presents difficult problems but also that things pertaining to society are more obscure than the things pertaining to nature. And yet, Simon notes, the object, method, and functions of modern social science have been allowed to be decided "quietly and painlessly, by dogmatic utterances, syllabi, postulations and semi-magical formulas," which "academic gentlemen," in the worst tradition of *scholasticism* as opposed to *science*, have allowed to assume the role of principles.[29] And among these postulates and formulas, none appears more firmly entrenched in the mainstream social science than that of "value neutrality." Social scientists must, it is asserted, refrain in their studies from "value judgments" lest they violate the indispensable standard of the true scientific method developed in the natural sciences. In itself, that is an excellent rule, because strict objectivity is a requirement for any rational inquiry. But if "social science" is to be recognized as a legitimate, autonomous branch of knowledge, the application of that rule needs to be clarified.

Simon begins by drawing our attention to what the term "value" as commonly used today stands for. Today "value" is generally understood not as something residing in things, but rather as something *attributed* to things, or processes. This attribution is found equally in idealist philosophies, political liberalism, and free-market economics, where it is virtually synonymous with subjective preference. Such subjective "values," Simon fully agrees, have no place in any rational studies, including the science of society. But this rule of exclusion changes radically, if "value" is understood realistically as a quality residing in the things themselves. Indeed, value so understood constitutes a concept no less essential in some studies of nature than in the study of society. Quantum mechanics may be a difficult case, but everyone recognizes that, say, the notion of "health" as a value present, or absent, in their specific subjects is what makes for intelligibility in botany and biology, as well as in medical studies, including psychology. Likewise, "healthy economy" or "healthy society" are clearly more than just metaphors of attribution in economics and sociology. What makes sense, common and professional, of depression or inflation, of *anomie* or juvenile delinquency, is the absence of something desirable, valuable, that is supposed to be "out there" in the economy or in society but happens to be missing.

Since the requirement for value neutrality in social studies is usually attributed to Max Weber, Simon wants us to know exactly why Weber recommends it. Weber is concerned about the exaggerated claims of Comtean positivism, and he wants to make it absolutely clear that no matter how advanced, social science will never be able to tell us *what* we have to do. Social science may give us options, but it will not and cannot choose a particular course of action for us. So that is one sense of its value-neutrality. But Weber also wants to impress upon his students the need for patience, hard work, and an *open mind* in the investigation of social subjects. Explaining *The Methodology of the Social Sciences*, Weber puts it as follows:

> The student should obtain, from his teacher in the lecture hall, the capacity: (1) to fulfill a given task in a workmanlike fashion; (2) definitely to recognize facts, even those which may be personally uncomfortable, and to distinguish them from his own evaluations; (3) to subordinate himself to his task and to repress the impulse to exhibit his personal tastes or other sentiments unnecessarily.[30]

Simon agrees with Weber on all these counts. Many people, he writes, turn to social studies "with a disorderly covetousness for judgments in terms of right and wrong." Such impatience and misdirected practical mindedness, he writes, "jeopardize experimental investigations as well as rational analysis."[31] The social scientists delude themselves, if they expect their research to provide specific answers about what is to be done. But they will also remain confused, if they insist on trying blindly to follow the allegedly unique scientific method developed in the natural sciences. The science of society differs from the science of physical phenomena in at least one decisive respect. Its investigations open to the human world where things can be otherwise than they are. As Aristotle puts it, while fire burns in the same way in Persia as in Greece, the Persians and the Greeks practice different ethics, economics, and politics.[32] In the language of the Aristotelian-Thomist epistemology, what makes the difference between learning about society and learning about nature is that what causes are to effects in nature, goals are to action in the human world. Within the given material circumstances, human events are understood as such, as human events, only with reference to a purpose. Modern physical sciences, relying in their research ever more on mathematics, may not need a "final cause" to explain their conclusions. But eliminating purpose makes for rather awkward reporting of human events. For instance, everybody understands that Frederick Jackson Turner's famous argument that "American democracy was born of no theorist dream. . . . It came out of the American forest" is not to be taken literally.[33] The frontier is an important factor in American history, but Philadelphia is much more explanatory. Things do happen, but human things, human events, are also made to happen, which for better or worse makes a difference. With still unsurpassed brevity and realism, Aristotle explains what is here at stake as follows: The city comes into being for the sake of sheer life, but it continues in being for the sake of good life.[34] The first stage is natural and inevitable, but the second clearly presents a choice and demands action.

Democracy is indeed one of the "phenomena" of modern history. But neither its meaning nor its practice can be explained exclusively with reference to "social and historical forces." The challenge now before the whole world is the one which Hamilton put to the American people in the first paragraph of *The Federalist* No. 1: To decide by their conduct "the important question of whether mankind [is] really capable of establishing good government from *reflection and choice* [italics supplied], or whether they are forever destined to depend for their political constitutions on accident and force." To explain how truly realistic that challenge is calls for nothing less than an ontology of practical knowledge.

SCIENCE AND PRACTICAL WISDOM

Ever since Plato, some philosophers and social scientists have speculated that Science, with capital S, may provide unique solutions to all human problems individual and social. And ever since Aristotle, other philosophers have insisted that in order not just to know what needs to be done but also to do it, we need more than just science. In order to act as we should, we need good will as well as right reason. Or to put it in another way, we act not just according to what we know but also according to who we are. And that is why in order to arrive at the right decision, and to act upon it, we need temperance, courage, justice, and prudence. In possession of these qualities, a person may be relied upon to do the right thing. But to acquire these qualities is not so easy, and the search for alternative solutions to social and personal problems never stops.

Simon identifies three modern examples of such "substitutes for virtues": the notion of natural spontaneity and goodness of man, the idea of social engineering, and last but not least, psychoanalysis.[35] For example, alleging that modern man has been spoiled by civilization, Rousseau urges a "return to Nature," to some pristine and innocent human condition. There are echoes here of the story of Eden, as well as of the stories of the noble savage peddled by some world travelers in Rousseau's time. Another version of a return to primitive goodness as solution to human problems is promoted by Emerson, who is so taken with spontaneity that he believes that "our moral nature is vitiated by any interference of our will." Emerson has no praise for those who struggle to acquire virtues. "We love characters," he writes, "in proportion as they are impulsive and spontaneous. The less a man thinks or knows about his virtues, the better we like him."[36] And though chastened somewhat by modern horrors, the belief in the natural goodness of man has by no means been totally extinguished.

Among the proponents of social engineering as the solution to all human problems, Simon picks Charles Fourier as the most outspoken and colorful. Aspiring to become the Newton of social science, Fourier proposes to organize society in accordance with the principle of "passional attraction," a kind of social gravity, as it were, that will allow every kind of human inclination to be expressed without disturbing overall social harmony. Fourier wants to gather similarly disposed people in more or less self-sufficient and specially designed buildings called Phalansteries (from monastery and phalanx). Thus people preferring monogamous marriage will have their own building, as will those preferring polygamy, or polyandry, or "free love," etc. Moreover, within each of these units, other preferences will be satisfied as well. For instance, the daily bread will be taken out of the oven at stated intervals so as to accommodate everyone's taste, and sewers would be cleaned by boys who like to play in the dirt. Eccentric and even silly as some of his plans are, they only confirm Fourier's absolute conviction that all human problems can be solved by clever "social engineering." And Simon duly recalls that far from dismissing him as a crank, Marx in *The Communist Manifesto* lists Fourier as an important Utopian Socialist.[37]

But finally, there is also modern "psycho-technology," which promises, or at least implies, that people may be able to get by, and along, without having to acquire temperance, courage, justice, and prudence. The need for character building and moral counsel is in this approach replaced by a kind of medical help. Unhappiness and behavioral problems which complicate people's lives, it is claimed, are amenable to treatment by psychoanalysis. Their origin can be traced to traumatic but suppressed childhood experiences, which the psychoanalyst must pry from the patient's subconscious. And once these traumas are brought up, recognized, and acknowledged by the patient, he or she may be expected to regain inner peace and to behave from then on in socially acceptable ways.[38]

Simon is critical of the naive reductionism in all of these "substitutes for virtues," but he does not overlook the genuine insights at their core. For instance, spontaneity, so extravagantly praised by Emerson, does improve, all other things being equal, both education and politics. Likewise, while Fourier's type of micromanagement is absurd, Simon is convinced that modern democratic society in order to operate properly needs to invest a great deal in constitutional organization. And finally, since they do often help people to "find themselves," Simon recognizes modern psychological techniques as both significant scientific breakthroughs and helpful social practice. In fact, he even envisages the possibility of new drugs doing, in specific cases, a better job of helping people than either psychoanalysis or moral counsel. But no matter how much reliance on spontaneity, rational social planning, and psychological help may contribute to the improvement of the quality of life, individual and social, they are clearly not enough. A normal or sane person is not the same as a good person; mere structural organization can never of itself maintain a just society; and natural spontaneity reduced to primitive instinct is hardly likely to produce such a society either. Simon suspects that the popularity of these modern substitutes for virtue comes from the people's reluctance to "pay the high price" of the effort required to develop a steady state of character that would guarantee their always doing the right thing by themselves as well as by society. Everyone knows from personal experience that resisting temptations, overcoming fear, and being fair are not always easy. But imagine a society where the majority of citizens have acquired these qualities. Wouldn't that tend to reduce many social problems? And is not that more realistic than to expect these problems to be solved in effect without people's conscious participation?

In his account of practical knowledge, Simon draws freely from Aristotle, but he also adds some helpful clarifications. So how does practical knowledge differ from the theoretical and the technical knowledge? How best can we distinguish prudence from science and art? As Simon explains it, all these types of knowledge possess a kind of reliability, a kind of readiness, but not of the same kind. Scientific and technical knowledge are characterized merely by what Simon calls *qualitative* readiness, which means simply that, if one has mastered a science or an art, one is qualified to practice it—if one cares to do so and for whatever purpose one chooses. This is the condition that Simon sometimes describes also as intellectual "habitus": the ability is there at the discretion, as it were, of its possessor. For instance, a talented artist may illustrate books for children, try a hand at counterfeiting, or even give up drawing altogether. A grammarian, Aristotle says, can make the best grammatical mistakes. Or as Simon notes, a good chemical engineer would be most qualified to sabotage a chemical plant. Whatever they are called, qualities such as artistic talent and scientific knowledge do not assure that even their most competent possessors will actually use them, or that they will use them properly. And this is precisely how the reliability of science or art differs from that of prudence. The reliability of practical wisdom, supported by the rest of the moral virtues, is not merely qualitative; it is both qualitative and *existential*. A prudent person will not only never act foolishly, a courageous person will never act cowardly, a temperate person intemperately, or a just person unjustly; in possession of these virtues, a person will also never fail to act, when action is indicated. There is no abstention from virtue. Or as Saint Augustine puts it, virtue is a quality of character that admits of no wrong use.[39] Virtues guarantee both their use and their right use.

Simon of course knows that "nobody is perfect," and he explicitly states that virtues admit of degrees and may be possessed in various proportions to each other. Moral virtues are personal qualities of character of unique individuals, and "we are all different." Proportions of temperance, courage, and justice will be balanced differently in equally decent and reliable people. Twin brothers may organize their families' lives in totally different yet morally equivalent ways. There is no unique prescription for how to bring up children that all parents must follow automatically. Moral goodness is, like love, "a many-splendored thing" that allows plenty of choices. Still, in order to become reliable, to become a good person, parent, or citizen, one needs to work on acquiring all moral virtues. Only practice makes perfect.

THE HEART OF DECISION MAKING

Rather than preaching morality, Simon is here expounding the theory of practical knowledge. That knowledge addresses "things that can be otherwise than they are," and he wants to explain why and how we decide to do this rather than that in any given, existentially unique situation. Thus, opening his discussion with a simple example, Simon invites us to imagine a vacationer in Switzerland. The man has climbed a few mountains in his time and is familiar with all the arguments for and against mountain climbing. He is no longer active, but one morning he is invited to join a group of mountaineers in scaling a particularly interesting summit that he had at one time considered climbing but never had the opportunity to climb. Before he responds to the invitation, the man clearly has to give it some thought. Especially because he knows all about mountain climbing, he will want to check the list of the party members, the reputation of the guide, the conditions not just of the "equipment" but of every single piece of it, the weather prognosis and, as the saying goes, a hundred other details, including his present family status and obligations. When he finally decides, "Yes, let us go," he has made an "ultimate practical judgment."[40]

Existentially unique in each case, this judgment is what practical wisdom or decision making is all about, and the example allows Simon to distinguish its main features rather clearly. For one thing, there is obviously something synthetic in this kind of judgment. The decision depends on putting together information about an indefinite number of disparate things, each of which may well be equally important: a frayed rope, a reckless fellow climber, a threatening storm, could each easily cause a fatal accident. But the "ultimate practical judgment" is synthetic also in another and more important sense. In deciding to do this rather than that, what is joined together are two indeed very different things, namely, thought and action. As Simon explains it, the ultimate practical judgment is not just very close to the action it brings about but is an inextricable part of it. In fact, the ultimate practical judgment is the "form" of the action: it makes the action to be this rather than that. It makes a difference between Yes and No! In the ultimate practical judgment, thought and action are literally fused together in a unique synthesis of realization.[41]

Forever thorough in his expositions, Simon acknowledges that synthesis is a method often used also in science and philosophy, and he specifically cites holism, vitalism, Gestalt theory, intuitionism of various descriptions, pragmatism, *Karakterkunde*, the stream of consciousness of William James, the deep self of Bergson, the existentialism of Sartre, all of which use synthetic approaches of one kind or another. Contemporary epistemology, he notes, is crowded with references to many operations of synthetic and constructive nature that are constantly performed by theoretical sciences. But none of these operations matches or even resembles the kind of synthesis effected in practical judgments. "Whether it sets things apart or puts them together," Simon writes, "theoretical thought remains primarily concerned with explanatory knowledge, i.e., with the analysis of effects and consequences into causes and principles."[42] The ultimate practical judgment, however, does not end in a conclusion; it results in action.

But the difference between theoretical speculation and explanation and the practical knowledge issuing in action goes even deeper. In contrast to strictly scientific procedures, objects of desire mix with objects of cognition at the very beginning of deliberation on what to do. Practical thinking does not work with just facts to construct its propositions; it always considers facts with regard to human wants and preferences. And that is why, in practical deliberations no less than in the ultimate practical judgment, over and above the facts of the situation, the character of the person or persons involved makes all the difference. To arrive at a correct theoretical conclusion, scientists can not only afford to hold certain things equal, abstract from others, even exclude a detail or two; they may also be arrogant, selfish, devious, contemptible characters and still come up with the right answer. By contrast, considering again Simon's example, we realize that to accept the invitation to climb that mountain in a rash response to a dare would be a wrong decision, comparable to ignoring a coming storm or not checking the equipment. Prudent is as prudent does.

TRUTH IN ACTION

What remains to be explained is the difference between what constitutes a correct theoretical conclusion in the sciences and what constitutes the right decision arrived at by prudence. In the realist view of the world and of its content, a scientific proposition is true if it corresponds to the facts. But that very realism recognizes a different necessary correspondence for the truth of the ultimate practical judgment. In the Thomistic vocabulary, the truth of practical knowledge is defined as the agreement between "right reason" and "good will." And Simon again explains what that means with a simple example. After careful deliberation about cost, timing, convenience, accident statistics, etc., a father decides that the family should take the train rather than drive or fly to go on vacation. But there is a wreck, and a child is killed. Can we say, after the fact, that the father's decision was wrong, or false, in the first place? Of course not. The man had arrived at his decision with the best interest of the family on his mind and in his heart and in accord with the best information about travel opportunities available. And given that agreement, his judgment was right and true and remains such forever after as the rule of action.[43] We cannot control every twist and turn that life has in store for us. But we are not entirely helpless when it comes to preparing ourselves to face those contingencies. The best "life and accident insurance," as it were, is the combination of intelligence and character. For all we really can ever do is to do the best we know how and the best we are able. Knowing more facts in any given situation is always useful, but that information of itself can neither tells us specifically what we ought to do, nor guarantee that no accidents will happen. We should never disregard facts, but we always act in accordance with who we are.

Keeping theoretical and practical knowledge distinct, then, is good, realistic epistemology. But in the present context we should note that to do so is good also for democracy. Since the practice of government by the consent of the governed depends clearly at least as much on the character of the governed as on their intelligence, holding up scientific procedures as the model for democratic decision making is not very helpful. For instance, Rawls suggests that democrats would do well to follow the pattern of "the common understanding and conclusions reached in the sciences." The best way to proceed, he writes, is "to assess theories and hypotheses in the light of the evidence by publicly recognized principles." Rawls does not mention character as a factor in practical decision making. But he does casually add that with "everyone taking counsel with himself, and with reasonableness, comity, and good fortune, it often works out well enough."[44] Now good fortune is always helpful. But comity, "social harmony," cannot be assumed as a given in any society, and perhaps least in democracy where everyone "takes counsel with himself." The "reasonableness" that makes for comity is less an IQ score than a character trait. Science cannot make democracy work. Democracy is the work of prudence.

Simon makes it absoltely clear that no science, no theory, no logical deduction can tell us what is the right thing to do in a given existential situation. The ultimate practical judgment is not arrived at by argument, by "assessing theories and hypotheses in the light of evidence." In the last analysis, each of us decides what to do or not do according to his or her own personal inclinations, character, virtues. Using the vocabulary of the philosophical tradition in which he works, Simon puts it as follows:

> The intellect, here, is the disciple of love. The object of practical judgment is one that cannot be grasped by looking at it. It is delivered by love to the docile intellect. As John of St. Thomas says in words of Augustinian beauty, *Amor transit in conditionem objecti*, "Love takes over the role of the object."[45]

Simon's language here may not sound "realistic," but it refers to real experience, to existential realities. Simon explains why we do what we do. We choose what we love because of who we are. And what he establishes is no monopoly of Aristotelian-Thomism. For here is what the founder of pragmatism, William James, has to say about it:

> *"Will you or won't you have it so?"* is the most probing question we are ever asked; we are asked it every hour of the day, and about the largest as well as the smallest . . . practical things. We answer by *consents or non-consents* and not by words. What wonder that these dumb responses should seem our deepest organs of communication with the nature of things! What wonder if the effort demanded by them be the measure of our worth as men! What wonder if the amount which we accord of it were the one strictly underived and original contribution which we make to the world![46]

James describes these consents and non-consents which determine our actions in existentially unique practical situations as "dumb." For Simon, the ultimate practical judgment, inasmuch as it admits of no strict derivation from general premises, is in fact incommunicable.[47] But personal as our specific decisions must be, this does not mean that practical knowledge lacks intelligible content. Its theory, as it were, recognizes that the original contribution we make to the world is the product of our reason and will. And that contribution, as everyone will acknowledge, is the true measure of our worth as human beings. In our relations to fellow citizens and the community itself, we can do what we do out of spite, for revenge, just to show off, or for profit, etc. But we can also do it out of love for justice, if we have enough courage.

In other words, Simon and James agree that in the construction of social reality what really matters is not so much our intelligence as our character. It is Simon, however, who supplies the final specification of practical knowledge in its requisite social context. What society is primarily interested in, Simon writes, is the actual *fulfillment* of what rules of behavior are on hand; society is less interested in the full *explanation* of these rules. In fact, as famously illustrated by the trial of Socrates, because serious inquiries into matters of morality and justice often raise more questions than they provide answers for, such investigations easily appear to threaten the socially necessary fulfillment of rules of behavior. To the democratically assembled Athenians, Socrates' incessant search for the meaning of justice appeared to impair the indispensable social order.[48] And to think of it, this fear may well be involved in the deposing of philosophical speculations by the contemporary defenders of democracy quoted at the beginning of this chapter.

Why else would Skinner want to move beyond "freedom and dignity," if not because philosophers have forever quarreled about their meaning? Reichenbach may doubt his own existence, as a philosopher, but as a citizen he insists that is "imbued with the essence of democracy." Rorty says he does not care much about reality but insists that democracy comes first. And Rawls wants to protect working democracy by isolating it from all "search for truth about an independent metaphysical and moral order." Now, as suggested above, there may be several reasons why these philosophers feel that they have to defend their commitment to democracy *against* their philosophy. But Simon's distinction between the fulfillment and the explanation of social rules points to an exonerating motive for their stand. Reichenbach, Rorty, Rawls, and others want, above all, democracy to work. They are looking for an "overlapping political consensus." And when they find no support for it in their philosophies, they are willing to set those philosophies aside. But Simon does not have to renege on his philosophy to honor his commitment to democracy. On the contrary, the Thomist realist metaphysics and epistemology, which recognize several kinds as well as degrees of knowledge, make it possible for Simon to embrace democracy honestly as the regime best suited to fulfill our rational as well as political nature. Simon has no problem endorsing the priority of fulfillment over explanation, which is not exactly the same as priority of democracy over philosophy. Plainly, society cannot stand still while philosophers labor to demonstrate the very last principle of liberty, equality, and fairness. But Simon can also remind us that no human fulfillment, and especially such a lofty achievement as a free government of the people, for the people, and by the people, can be said to be actually fulfilled without adequate explanation. Social life must go on, and necessarily so, on the basis of habit, customs, and ideological substitutes for philosophy. Moreover, what needs to be done in unique contingent situations will always be decided not by logical deduction from theoretical premises but by good will in support of right reason. From a practical point of view, then, all other things being equal, rules of behavior may well be safer in people's hearts than in their minds. As Madison wisely notes, "even the most rational government will not find it a superfluous advantage to have the prejudices of the community on its side."[49] But none of this absolves the philosopher from striving to clarify all the factors that go into the making of the right decisions. For as Simon puts it, "understanding and explanation are perfections that matter for proper fulfillment in the life of rational agents."[50]

Necessary fulfillment of social rules must go on with the help of what understanding of them is available at any given time. Moreover, no utopia, democratic, scientific, or any other kind, lies in the future. Human progress in anything is slow, gradual, and exposed to all sorts of contingencies, not excluding dramatic reversals. The best we can expect from democracy is a conscious approximation to its stated ideals. And that is why separating efforts to maintain and improve democratic practice from serious philosophical inquiries seems such a strange advice, to say nothing about pretending that "to know the world and its content" does not really matter. With greater respect for the political and rational nature of mankind, Simon takes a different stand. He believes that the best way to promote democratic freedom and dignity is to promote a cultural environment "in which moral philosophy is no longer seen as the thing that threatens to cripple resolution and to endanger society."[51]

NOTES

1. Hans Reichenbach, *The Rise of Scientific Philosophy* (Berkeley: University of California Press, 1951), p. 61.

2. Ibid., p. 268.

3. B. F. Skinner, *Beyond Freedom and Dignity* (New York: Knopf, 1971).

4. Skinner, "On 'Having' a Poem," *Saturday Review* (July 15, 1972): 32–35.

5. John R. Searle, *The Construction of Social Reality* (New York: Free Press, 1995), xiii.

6. Ibid., p. 157.

7. Ibid., p. 219.

8. Ibid., p. 228.

9. Ibid.

10. Richard Rorty, "The Priority of Democracy to Philosophy," in *The Virginia Statute for Religious Freedom*, ed. Merrill D. Peterson and Robert C. Vaughan (Cambridge: Cambridge University Press, 1988).

11. See D. Vanden House, *Without God or His Double: Realism, Relativism, and Rorty* (Leiden, Netherlands: E. J. Brill, 1994), p. 1.

12. See "There is No Big Picture," interview with Richard Rorty, "a world-

famous philosopher," in *The University of Chicago Magazine*, vol. 68, no. 4 (April 1994), pp. 19–23.

13. Quoted in David A. Hall, *Richard Rorty: Prophet and Poet of the New Pragmatism* (Albany: State University of New York Press, 1994), p. 18.

14. Ibid.

15. See Konstantin Kolenda, *Rorty's Humanistic Pragmatism: Philosophy Democratized* (Tampa, FL: Universitiy of South Florida Press, 1990).

16. Rorty, "Priority of Democracy," p. 268.

17. John Rawls, "Justice as Fairness: Political Not Metaphysical," *Philosophy and Public Affairs*, vol. 17 (1988), p. 230.

18. John Rawls, "The Priority of Right and Ideas of the Good," *Philosophy and Public Affairs*, vol. 17, no. 3 (1988), p. 259.

19. What makes Rorty's and Rawls's intellectual predicament especially intriguing is that the philosophers who they say inspired them, and whose teaching they presumably want to improve, namely Kant and Dewey, certainly do not oppose philosophical search for truth to political justice or to democracy as the preferred regime.

20. "All our freedom," Simon insists, "is contained within limits of our knowledge of truth." *Community of the Free* (New York: Henry Holt, 1947), p. 4.

21. Jacques Maritain, *The Degrees of Knowledge: Distinguish to Unite* (Notre Dame, IN: University of Notre Dame Press, 1995), pp. 41–50. The French original was published in 1932, the English translation under the supervision of Gerald B. Phelan in 1959. We leave out its Second Part dealing with "The Degrees of Suprarational Knowledge."

22. Aristotle, *Ethics* 1.2.1094^{b}5.

23. See Thomas S. Kuhn, *The Structure of Scientific Revolutions* (Chicago, IL: University of Chicago Press, 1962). A second enlarged version of this book was published in 1972 as Volume II, Number 2, of an International Encyclopedia of Unified Science, edited by Otto Neurath, Rudolph Carnap, and Charles Morris. This Encyclopedia project was sponsored by the Foundation for the Unity of Science, which has since been dissolved.

24. Aristotle, *On the Soul* 3.8.431^{b}22. Interestingly enough, Kuhn concedes that his account leaves open the question, "What must the world be like in order that man may know it?" *Scientific Revolutions*, p. 173.

25. Simon elaborates on this topic in *Metaphysics of Knowledge*, p. 142ff.

26. The confusion about the objectivity of science was recently highlighted by Alan D. Sokal when he revealed that his article "Transgressing the Boundaries—Toward a Transformative Hermeneutics of Quantum Gravity," published in *Social Texts* (Spring/Summer 1996), was a deliberate hoax. Quoting appropriate postmodernist writers, Sokal in his article raises mock-profound questions

about our ability to know for real the world and its content, which apparently suited the deconstructionist bias of the editors, who rushed to publish it without submitting it to expert reviews. In one of the many commentaries on "Sokal's Hoax," Steven Weinberg, Sokal's fellow scientist, wants it to be known that even though the objective nature of scientific knowledge is denied by some scientists (e.g., Andrew Ross and Bruno Latour), and by some philosophers (e.g., Richard Rorty and Thomas Kuhn), the reality of the world and the objectivity of scientific knowledge are taken for granted by most natural scientists. *The New York Review of Books* (August 8, 1996), pp. 11–15.

27. Yves R. Simon, "Maritain's Philosophy of the Sciences," in Jacques Maritain, *The Philosophy of Nature* (New York: Philosophical Library, 1951), pp. 157–82. See also Simon, *The Great Dialogue of Nature and Space* [Aristotle vs. Descartes], ed. Gerald J. Dalcourt (Albany, NY: Magi Books, 1970); and *Foresight and Knowledge*, tr. Ralph Nelson and Anthony O. Simon (New York: Fordham University Press, 1996); the French original, *Prevoir et savoir*, was published by Éditions de l'Arbre in Quebec in 1944.

28. Simon, "Philosophy of the Sciences," p. 169.

29. Yves R. Simon, *Practical Knowledge*, ed. Robert J. Mulvaney (New York: Fordham University Press, 1991), p. 115.

30. Ibid., p. 136n16.

31. Ibid., p. 130.

32. Artistotle, *Ethics* 6.2.1139^{a}21.

33. Frederick Jackson Turner, *The Frontier in American History* (New York: Henry Holt, 1920), p. 293.

34. Artistotle, *Politics* 1.2.1252^{b}29.

35. Yves R. Simon, *The Definition of Moral Virtue*, ed. Vukan Kuic (New York: Fordham University Press, 1986), ch. 1.

36. Quoted in *Moral Virtue*, p. 7.

37. Ibid., pp. 9, 37.

38. Ibid., pp. 14–15.

39. Ibid., pp. 71–72, 78.

40. Yves R. Simon, *Practical Knowledge*, ed. Robert J. Mulvaney (New York: Fordham University Press, 1991), p. 3.

41. Ibid., p. 8.

42. Ibid., p. 7.

43. Ibid., pp. 21–23.

44. John Rawls, *A Theory of Justice* (Cambridge, MA: Harvard University Press, 1971), pp. 388–90.

45. *Practical Knowledge*, p. 18.

46. William James, *Psychology: The Briefer Course*, ed. Gordon Alport (New York: Harper Torch Books, 1952), p. 327. James parts ways with Thomism

when he suggests that our consents and non-consents determine not just our practical decisions but also our theoretical conclusions. The above quotation omits "the most theoretical things."

47. *Practical Knowledge*, p. 24.

48. Ibid., p. 35. Simon notes that the "traditionalistic movements which reacted against 18th century rationalism, the Nietzschean protest, and some aspects of pragmatism, all express the conviction that rational analysis, is, or may be, a threat to firmness of action."

49. Alexander Hamilton, John Jay, James Madison, *The Federalist* No. 49 (New York: Modern Library), p. 328.

50. *Practical Knowledge*, p. 37.

51. *Practical Knowledge*, p. 38.

3

LIBERTY AND AUTHORITY

Most people in democracy believe that the powers of government must be balanced by the rights of the citizens. Democratic rhetoric may favor the latter, but it is generally recognized that individual liberties, too, need to be limited, if there is to be law and order. Opposing political parties may disagree on which activities need to be checked, but they do not challenge the principle itself of ordered liberty and limited government. For instance, the conservatives advocate less regulation of business, but they would not mind some controls imposed on certain alternative lifestyles. And the liberals do the same the other way around. They call for stricter regulation of business but urge extension of personal choices. In short, while they may have preferences, both liberals and conservatives uphold the balance between liberty and authority as the mark of constitutional democracy.

Beneath this conventional view, however, there lurks an important and difficult issue of political theory. How exactly are liberty and authority related under democratic government? Because any extension of the power of government appears to encroach upon the freedom of the citizens, and vice versa, constitutional authority and liberty seem to stand in opposition to each other. But since democracy clearly needs both, liberty and authority must obviously be in some sense also complementary. Thus liberty and authority may be said to complement each other in constituting the necessary balance that keeps democracy from turning either into tyranny of the majority or collapsing into anarchy. An unchecked increase in authority threatens the former, unlimited expansion of liberty the latter, and history knows a few examples of each. The exact relation between liberty and authority, however, poses also a deeper theoretical question: Must any increase in one necessarily be at the expense of the other? We do not think either "free government" or "ordered liberty" to be contradictions in terms. Yet imagining them both expanding at the same time does present some conceptual difficulties. More government and more freedom at the same time? Most theorists of democracy prefer to stay with the concept of the balance of opposites.

Simon recognizes, of course, that in the hustle and bustle of everyday life and politics what people take for liberty and authority frequently generates conflict, which is best settled by trimming the claims of both in a judicious compromise. But as he carefully examines their meanings, Simon reveals for us also the more fundamental complementary relation between liberty and authority, which is especially relevant for democracy. He shows how under the surface of opposition, liberty and authority work together for the same end. In fact, in contrast to other forms of government, which set narrow limits to their cooperation, government of the people, for the people, and by the people has no specific limits regarding ways in which liberty and authority can support each other. In democracy, political liberty and political authority may expand together to make the system ever more democratic. Leaving conventional interpretations behind, Simon connects "ordered liberty" and "free government" in a unique interpretive synthesis.

CONCEPTS OF FREEDOM

Perhaps the best known current classification of theories of political liberty is Isaiah Berlin's distinction between Hobbes's "negative" and Rousseau's "positive" interpretations. Roughly, negative freedom is defined as absence of external obstacles to one's actions, while positive freedom is in effect identified with conformity to a preexisting standard, say, the General Will (which can "force one to be free").[1] Of course, as more or less sympathetic commentators on Berlin's thesis have pointed out, each side in this division contains several historical variants, some of which overlap across the line.[2] In the present context, however, let us merely note that given a strict choice between Berlin's two concepts, most people, of either conservative or liberal leanings, would likely pick negative liberty. Berlin does so himself. Absence of coercion promises more liberty than any kind of positive arrangements or requirements.

In the more elaborate classification of basic notions of liberty presented by Mortimer Adler, one's choice might not be so easy. According to Adler, who constructs his scheme from a comprehensive survey of the entire history of Western political thought, at one time or another liberty had been conceived as: 1. "circumstantial freedom of self-realization" (e.g., Voltaire, Hume, J. S. Mill, Hayek); 2. "acquired freedom of self-perfection" (e.g., Plato, Marcus Aurelius, Spinoza); and 3. "natural freedom of self-determination" (e.g., Descartes, William James, Bergson, Sartre). However, there are also combinations of these basic definitions. For instance, some thinkers combine the first two notions (e.g., Freud, Russell); others the first and the third (e.g., Adam Smith, Burke); and still others the second and the third (e.g., Augustine, Luther, Rousseau, Whitehead). Additionally, Adler lists "political liberty" as a special variant of circumstantial self-realization, and "collective freedom" as a special variant of acquired self-perfection.[3] Had Berlin been acquainted with Simon's teaching, he would have had trouble placing him in either his "negative" or his "positive" category.[4] Adler has a greater choice and, after quoting at length from his writings, groups Simon together with Aquinas, Locke, Montesquieu, and Maritain, all of whom are said to subscribe to all of the above notions of freedom except "collective freedom" (which is said to be advocated by Bakunin, Comte, Marx, Nietzsche, and Saint-Simon).[5]

Now "the celebrated" Montesquieu, as the authors of *The Federalist* call him, is indeed a theorist whose definitions of political liberty and of free government provide solid support for the concept of constitutional democracy (even though he himself preferred constitutional monarchy). Political liberty, Montesquieu explains, is "the right of doing whatever the laws permit," for if people were allowed to do what the laws forbid, no one would be free. But such liberty under law will be safe only under a "free government," which Montesquieu defines as one under which "no man shall be compelled to do things to which law does not oblige him, nor be forced to abstain from things which the law permits." Put together, these two definitions affirm that "in societies directed by laws, liberty can consist only in the power of doing what we ought to will, and in not being constrained to do what we ought not to will."[6] In Adler's terms, then, Montesquieu sees political liberty under a free government to consist in the individuals' self-determination, self-realization, and self-perfection under the rule of law. Simon would have no reason to object to these definitions, but in his writings he never refers to Montesquieu. Instead, with reference to what he considers to be some dominant influences in contemporary thinking, harking all the way back to philosophical speculations in ancient Greece, he offers a classification of views of freedom different from both Berlin's and Adler's.

The "gratuitous act" beloved of existentialist literature is, according to Simon, the perfect literary expression of a theory found in a variety of philosophical, moral, scientific, and psychological contexts, which from the consideration that causal or deterministic processes are predictable infers that the real measure of our freedom is unpredictability.[7] For example, in one of André Gide's novels, a character throws a perfect stranger from a speeding train for no reason except to prove, "on the spur of the moment," his total freedom. For a less ominous example of freedom conceived as something without a determined cause, Simon cites a few lines from René de Chateaubriand's *Voyage en Amérique*. A Rousseauean romantic (pace Berlin), Chateaubriand found in the American wilderness what he was looking for: "Many boast of loving liberty, yet almost no one has a proper understanding of it . . . [Here] going from tree to tree; to the right and to the left indifferently, I was saying to myself: here, there are no more roads to be followed, no more cities, no more narrow homes, no more presidents, republics or kings, above all, no more laws." He felt, Chateaubriand wrote, "free as a bird."[8]

Taking a longer historical view, we discover that freedom as something indeterminate and unpredictable may well have been first conceived, at a deeper level, by Epicurus looking as a moralist for an escape from the atomic determinism of Democritus. "Better to follow the myths about gods," Epicurus complains, "than to become a slave to the destiny of the natural philosophers; for the former suggests a hope of placating the gods by worship, whereas the latter involves a necessity which knows no placation." Leaving gods aside, Epicurus solves his problem by introducing in his physics an absolutely unpredictable swerve in the rain of atoms, *clinamen*, that not only explains the diversity of things but also affirms the existence of human freedom. Lucretius puts it as follows: "But that the very mind feels not some necessity within it doing all things, and is not constrained like a conquered thing to bear and suffer, this is brought about by the tiny swerve of the first-beginnings in no determined direction of place and at no determined time." And interestingly enough, as modern physics abandoned the strict Newtonian determinism, speculation about freedom as something indeterminate and unpredictable appeared to find once again confirmation in the preeminent intellectual discipline of the age, nuclear physics. Thus commenting, not entirely tongue-in-cheek, on Heisenberg's discovery of the "principle of indeterminacy," A. S. Eddington suggests that physicists can now finally understand what is meant by freedom.[9] For Simon, however, it makes as little sense to equate human freedom with indeterminism as to speak of the indeterminate or unpredictable behavior of individual atomic particles as being "free."

According to Simon, the problem with most attempts to deal with this perennial human subject is that they assume determinism and indeterminism to be the exclusive alternatives in ethics and politics no less than in physics. But in the human world of deliberation and action, those are not the only choices. The third alternative and the true opposite of indeterminism is precisely our freedom of choice, which is best understood as *superdetermined*.

Radically condensed, Simon's argument runs as follows. The basic precondition for the freedom of choice is an "active indifference" toward the alternatives available. In this state of active indifference, we see a choice among specific particular goods or ends, and we are tempted to think that we may choose among them at will. But this assumes that the alternatives we face are in themselves all equal, which is far from self-evident. Facing a moral dilemma, we are not about to toss a coin. We want to make the right choice. And as everyone knows, being able to do so is not easy.

What Simon means by freedom of choice being superdetermined may be here illustrated by one of his only apparently simple examples. In a convivial group, I yield to the temptation to tell a truly funny but rather uncharitable and potentially damaging story about a mutual acquaintance. Have I done the right thing? Most people will probably agree that what I did was not nice, and some might even suspect that my choice to tell the story might not have been altogether free. Simon has no doubts about it. Voluntary and even "free," in a weak sense, this choice fails the true test of superdetermination. Whatever fleeting pleasure I may have derived from attracting attention by my malicious gossip, I have thereby done harm to a fellow human being. I have violated charity, which is so basic to proper human relations. I was not able to resist an all too human temptation. Had I been capable of "superdetermination," I would have chosen to keep my mouth shut.

Real life situations are usually more complex, subtle, serious, and obscure than the above example, and it may very well be that no one has ever known anyone who had never made a wrong moral choice. But recognizing that no one is perfect and that human life is full of contingencies only confirms the need for superdetermination in our doing the right thing. We choose freely only when we choose to do the right thing. When we do the wrong thing, don't we like to say that we do not know what came over us? It is thus by acknowledging our imperfections that we can best understand what Simon means by superdetermination. The true freedom of choice, he writes, "proceeds not from any weakness, any imperfection, any feature of potentiality on the part of the agent but, on the contrary, from a plenitude of being and an abundance of determination."[10]

Again, real life moral choices are often difficult, and even decent people are bound on occasion to make a wrong choice. But the ultimate sense of true freedom of choice is not all that mysterious. If we are not coerced to it, our decision to take a particular course of action is properly described as voluntary. Are we entitled, without regard to what is chosen, to call it also a free decision? Many people would think so, because they believe that absence of external coercion is what defines true freedom. But reminded how wrong choices often appear more attractive, most would perhaps concede that it takes some effort to resist the easy way out. This is one way of recognizing true freedom of choice as a kind of superdetermination. Regardless of sacrifices, we choose freely only when we do right by our neighbors and our community as well as by ourselves. And in the present context, it seems hardly necessary to add that democracy is obviously the regime that stands to gain most from such understanding of the freedom of choice.

THE COMMON GOOD AND ITS COUNTERFEITS

Simon provides us with the second key to the complementary nature of political liberty and political authority by clarifying the meaning of the common good of society. In their current debates, the liberal and the communitarian writers both make reference to the "common good," but with multiple meanings assumed on both sides, their exchanges do not seem very helpful. It is worth noting, however, that even though the communitarians do not interpret the "commom good" uniformly, neither do the liberals deny its relevance for democracy.[11] Because Simon holds firmly the good of the human community to be greater than the good of the same order of any of its parts, one may be tempted to classify him as a communitarian. But since he also insists that individual rights and liberties are integral parts of the common good of society, Simon would seem to qualify also as a liberal. In fact, however, neither of these labels fits. Simon defends individual rights not against but in the name of the common good.[12]

According to Simon, the history of political thought reveals two main misinterpretations of the good of society. In one of these, the good of society is conceived after the pattern of a work of art and thus as something external to its members. In the other, the good of society is conceived as a mere means to the good of individuals. For a popular illustration of the first misconception one could point to the pyramids of Egypt, but far more insidious instances of this type of counterfeit common good are found in the theories of the transcendent state, from Plato to Hegel. In this model, the state is seen as a kind of masterwork of art, and because there is special satisfaction in handling its "material," endowed with intelligence and freedom, both men of action and political thinkers are attracted to it. "The finest clay," Nietzsche exalts, "the most precious marble—man—is here kneaded and hewn."[13] Indeed, just as teachers of history sometimes identify with heroes whose prowess they narrate to schoolchildren, Simon remarks, "so political thinkers derive enthusiasm from identification with the molders of cities and states."[14] *The Republic* may be a beautifully constructed model of the ideal community, but no one in it, guardian or producer, is free to choose life, liberty, and the pursuit of happiness on his or her own. Among the reasons Aristotle rejects Plato's politics, this is not the least.

Preoccupation with safeguarding the right to individual pursuit of happiness, however, has also lead to gross misrepresentation of the nature of the common good of society. As if reacting against the transcendent or "artistic" conceptions of it, some thinkers go to the other extreme. They either deny altogether that there is such a thing as *common* good, or they reduce it to nothing more than a means to the good of individuals. Friedrich A. Hayek supplies a particularly blunt statement of the latter position. Raising the question of whether government should use its power of taxation to finance such services as the care of the disabled and the provision of roads, Hayek questions whether "coercing people to contribute to the achievement of ends in which they are not interested can be morally justified." And the best he can do is to suggest that "most of us find it expedient to make such a contribution on the understanding that we will in turn profit from similar contributions of others toward the realization of our own ends."[15]

Lest this view be confused with libertarian-capitalist ideology, let it be noted that, however nuanced, doubts about the reality of the common good of society may be found also at the other end of the partisan spectrum. Simon quotes Harold Laski of the British Labor Party, who put it this way: "The surrender we make is a surrender not for the rights of society regarded as something other than its members, but exactly and precisely for men and women whose totality is conveniently summarized in a *collective and abstract noun*" (italics supplied).[16] In other words, only slightly different from Hayek's, Laski lets individuals trade with each other in surrenders rather than contributions. And in order to quash all possible claims on its behalf, Laski, a socialist, not only denies that the good of society has an independent existence but does not hesitate to reduce "society" itself to a convenient abstraction. "The nominalistic mind," Simon notes, "is as unable to grasp the reality of a community as it is unable to grasp the meaning of a universal nature."[17]

More recently, Robert A. Dahl has indulged similar doubts specifically with regard to the future development of democracy. "The general good of the city," Dahl writes, "can always be *decomposed* [italics supplied] into what is good for the persons in the community . . . [it] is not something different from the interests or the good of persons who compose the collectivity or are affected by it." Moreover, as he sees it, in order to "encompass the heterogenous attachments, loyalties, and beliefs" present in modern advanced democratic societies, even this sense of the general good has now been "stretched so thinly," Dahl writes, as to have no practical use. Thus the notion of the common good, according to Dahl, is today "but a poignant reminder of an ancient vision that irreversible change has made irrelevant to the conditions of modern and postmodern political life."[18]

Now the main reason why writers of such different political persuasions, Hayek, Laski, Dahl, are reluctant to acknowledge the real existence of a good belonging to the political association as such, distinct from the particular goods of its members, is clearly their concern for the rights and liberties of the individual citizens. They fear that recognizing a distinct common good might diminish the viability of those rights and liberties, and, recalling the abuses of the notion of the common good throughout history, theirs is certainly a legitimate concern. They know, of course, that "no man is an island." But they also know that power corrupts, and they do not want us to forget to what tragic extremes the invocation of the glory of a divine ruler, of a transcendent state, or of a classless society can lead. Thus distrusting political authority's claim to be in charge of the good of all, they want the latter to be "decomposable" into the good of each. The problem is that rejecting the common good as an "operational concept,"[19] tends to turn democratic society itself not into a convenient but a rather awkward abstraction.

Leaving aside the philosophical critique of the nominalist interpretation of universals and collective nouns, which makes it difficult for those who subscribe to it to acknowledge the real existence of society,[20] let us here stay with the ordinary, commonsense understanding of social experience and history. What about the ancient Egypt and its untold dynasties, and the four-thousand-year-old Chinese history? What about the Western, or Indian, or any other civilization? Was not the United States "born" on July 4, 1776, to "grow" in two hundred and some years into the preeminent world power (with all the problems that go with it)? Historical narrative is not about "convenient abstractions." Nations have meaningful real existence, as do families, teams, and orchestras (even forests and sandy beaches). Society is not just a collective noun; it is a collective experience. The failure to make the common good into an operational concept is traceable to a methodological as well political prejudice. For instance, their pretended scientific method forbids the behavioralists from speculating about what might be in people's hearts and minds. But as Simon points out, that is precisely the only place where real communities and their common good can be found. The common good of society is neither some brooding presence in the sky nor a physical datum. What makes and keeps communities together is the shared awareness of a common end-good that its members recognize as transcending their particular end-goods. This awareness constitutes the only real, existential, live common good. When members subjectively conclude that their living together no longer serves a higher, common end, communities fall apart, dissolve, divorce. Liberal political theorists may not be totally unaware of this sense of the common good, but they apparently feel that it is best, if not to deny it, to obscure it for the better protection of individual rights.

A careful reading of their texts, however, shows that even when they glorify individual liberty most, liberals cannot quite do without appealing to an unnamed common good. Liberal writers appreciate the benefits of community more than they care to admit. Thus no matter how nonjudgmental they try to be, when it is a question of individual tastes, opinions, and even behavior, liberals quickly turn dogmatic when the question is about relevant merits of different political regimes. The system that maximizes individual freedoms is good, the one that suppresses individual freedoms is unqualifiedly bad. But does not that mean that what distinguishes democracy from, say, fascism, is precisely the difference in their respective "joint human efforts that we call political?"[21] In other words, liberals assume that democracies pursue genuine common good, and they denounce fascism for trying to get away with a counterfeit. For they know that democratic freedom is as much a collective as a private good.

The notion of the common good as the good of the political association as a whole, distinct from the goods of its members, may also be elucidated with the generally accepted difference between a confederation and a federal union. The former is a sort of political partnership, somewhat closer than an alliance, but still not a true community, because its good is indeed decomposable, as Dahl would say, into the goods of its members. By contrast, a federation, representing "a more perfect union," is a full-fledged political association whose good is indeed common to all its member states and yet distinct from the sum of their own particular goods. Recall Socrates' suggestion that we should look for the meaning of justice in the city rather than in the individual, because in the city justice is "writ large." Looking at a federal union, we grasp the meaning of the common good more easily, because its constitution displays it in large letters, so to speak. States join together in federal unions in order to escape the uncertainties of the international "state of nature," and to preserve both their identity and their freedom. And barring unjust treatment, no State can conceive its own common good apart from the good of the union in which it partakes equally with all the other members, assured of the benefits of both domestic tranquility and common defense. Thus in contrast to the writers quote above, no student of modern federalism has ever argued that the good of the union is nothing but the sum total of the goods of its member states, or the greatest good of their greatest number.[22]

Aristotle calls the common good of the human association "divine," by which, as Simon points out, he wants to contrast the durability of society compared to the relatively short lives of individuals. Individuals come and go, but communities, from families, tribes, nations, and empires, not only last longer but are also unique carriers of human progress. The saying that Rome was not built in a day, which is true, is meant to convey the larger truth that all great human goods are collective goods, produced by joint efforts and distributed over periods dwarfing the short span of individual lifetimes. As Simon notes, schoolchildren today are able to solve mathematical problems which would have stymied Archimedes or Descartes.[23] Thus science no less than liberty or democracy is a common good, transcending the benefit particular individuals, in their time, may derive from any of them.

To reduce the good of society to a mere means to the good of individuals, then, is as wrong as to present it as a work of art, i.e., divorced from morality as well as from individual goods.[24] We arrive at the truth of the matter by rejecting both these errors and returning to some basic principles established already by Aristotle. The human species is by nature social, political, and rational. The city comes into being for the sake of life but continues in being for the sake of the good life. And the best such life, if you can have it, is one in which citizens take turns ruling and being ruled and in so doing have a chance to become both good citizens and good persons.[25] Now Aristotle may not have personally "believed" in democracy, but this rule based on his analysis of human nature fits perfectly the government of the people, for the people, by the people.

Socrates was wrong when he imagined the state as man writ large composed of *unequal* parts. And so was also Hobbes when he let his Leviathan be depicted as a divine-like giant composed of politically neutered manikins. The theoretically correct metaphor, so to speak, of the political association is a whole made in the image of its parts, which forever preserves its parts as wholes in their own right. Made in the image of its members, the political community is a real, rational, and moral being, alive in the hearts and minds of its members. In other words, a true polity will retain its proper name only so long as each and every one of its members is also recognized and treated as a unique whole, a real, rational, and moral being. The "right to privacy" appears today hopelessly enmeshed in confusing partisan politics and legal wrangling, but there is no question that the concept of democratic citizenship includes the notion of "inalienable rights." It is only that the specific reasons for taking these rights seriously are not always clearly explained. Defending civil rights exclusively out of concern and respect for individuals may be excusable as partisan strategy, but it represents nevertheless a gross theoretical error. A far more compelling reason, practical no less than theoretical, for defending each citizen's personal integrity arises out of the recognition of the true nature and the true good of the political community. Individuals indeed deserve respect, but even greater respect is due to the community that includes the protection of individual rights as part of its common good. And so, in contrast to the views cited above, Simon insists not just that the common good enjoys primacy over individual goods, of the same order, but also that this moral common good is realized only through continual distribution to all members of the community.[26]

People prefer democracy, because it is supposed to be such a community, and when they fight for their rights, they are in effect fighting to keep it such. But assuring the enjoyment of private rights can never be the whole of the common good of a democratic polity. John Locke has it right when he insists that "the rule and measure of *all* law making" is *the public good*.[27] The protection and promotion of individual rights does not exhaust what a democracy has to do in order to remain a real, rational, workable community. Democracy needs government in the first place precisely in order to be democracy.

THE DEFICIENCY THEORY OF GOVERNMENT

The history of the twentieth century is inseparable from the clash of three ideologies, liberal democracy, communism, and fascism, whose perceived and real differences loom large in its narrative. The First World War was supposed to make the world safe for democracy against old-fashioned authoritarian regimes. The Second World War, fought against fascism, was supposed to liberate mankind from fear and want and assure freedom of speech and religion to everyone. And the longest, if not the bloodiest, the so-called Cold War, continued that struggle against communism, which had replaced fascism as the main enemy of human freedom and decency. No matter how many other factors contributed to making the twentieth century eclipse other historical "times of trouble" in death and misery, the clash of these ideologies is decisive for the understanding of its history. Sadly, while people will fight for treasure and territory, they will fight even more fiercely over different interpretations of human nature and destiny. The battle between democracy, fascism, and communism may be looked at as a kind of secular equivalent of religious wars of yore. Still, just as in the case of religions, that does not mean that these ideologies do not have anything in common. What comes as a surprise, however, is what Simon finds they all agree upon. Simon calls it "the deficiency theory of government." Further political development in established democracies as well as the chances of stabilizing the conversion to democracy in the former communist states can both be helped by exposing the delusions of this popular theory.

The best known version of the deficiency theory of government is, of course, the Marxist doctrine of the withering away of the state. Marx and Engels argued that once private property is abolished and the class struggle comes to an end, the government of persons will be replaced by the administration of things, and the organized political authority of the state will be a thing of the past.[28] Utopian on its face, this doctrine was nevertheless kept alive by the Soviet Communist Party leadership almost until the very end. It was a part of Stalin's doctrine of socialism in one country, of Khrushchev's concept of the state of the whole people, and it even found echoes in Gorbachev's call for *glasnost* and *perestroika*. People tend to believe what they want or are made to believe, and this doctrine was definitely a factor in the popularity of communism throughout the world, now conveniently forgotten. The prospect of freedom from government, no matter how fantastic or remote, has universal human appeal.

In fact, a version of the deficiency theory of government played an important role both in the debates leading to the American Revolution and in the campaign for the ratification of the Constitution. And as the latest partisan politics illustrate, its appeal still resonates among the voters more than two hundred years later. Expressed in pithy language matching Engel's radical formula, examples of this liberal democratic version of the deficiency theory of government are found in both *The Common*

Sense and *The Federalist*, among other sources. Thus whereas Tom Paine proclaimed that "society is produced by our wants and government by our wickedness,"[29] Madison readily allows that "if men were angels, no government would be necessary."[30] The decisive difference here, of course, is that while Marx and Engels blame the need for government on the faulty organization of society, Paine and Madison trace it to a built-in weakness in human nature itself. And because human nature seems less amenable to change than social institutions, the final "withering away of the state," logically deductible from the Marxist premises, is not predicted in liberal theory. Liberal theory acknowledges that the government of persons is here to stay. But whether this is so only because "men are not angels" needs to be further examined.

That the fascists also subscribe to the deficiency theory of government is less obvious but no less certain. In contrast to Marxism and liberalism, which deprecate it, fascism exalts the power of the state. Indeed, rather than treating it as "a necessary evil," as some of Paine's ideological descendants still seem to do in this country, fascists worship the state as the supreme good. And yet, among the blasts and boasts of their rhetoric, one can spot a note of protest against human fate. Why do fascists insist on the strictest individual discipline and the strongest possible political authority? They do it because they too know that men are not angels. But instead of trying to make the best out of that given human condition by devising, say, balanced constitutions, fascists propose to put supermen in charge. Those who are able to overcome ordinary human weaknesses will be rulers and will keep the rest of mankind in their inferior places. And so, by making might right, the supermen will straighten what is wrong with the world.[31]

We see, then, how even as they start from different philosophical premises and propose different political solutions, the three major ideologies whose clashes explain much of the twentieth century nevertheless share one basic theoretical assumption. They all assume that the need for government is caused by the lack of some human excellence, by the need to correct one or another human deficiency. For the communists, this deficiency is private property and the division of societies into classes; for the fascists, it is the division of humanity into superior and inferior individuals as well as races; and for the liberals, it is the congenital human unreliabilty, if not also wickedness. And so, based on these beliefs, the communists dream about withering away of the state following the abolition of class divisions, and the fascists feel both superior and guiltless in lusting to dominate the rest of the world. Being by comparison less dogmatic about either the human nature or the nature of society, the liberals do not go for such final solutions. Instead, they prefer to experiment with political institutions that promise to compensate for the worst of human deficiencies. To rephrase a famous Madison's formula slightly out of context, liberals seek liberal remedies for the diseases most incident to liberal democracy. And as the record shows, they have been rather successful—at least up to now. On the eve of the next millennium, democracy appears to be everybody's (or almost everybody's) preferred regime. But as the conditions of life in common at all levels become more complicated, the question arises whether the liberal deficiency theory of government can sustain the democratic experiment which has now expanded onto a global scale. Never truly convincing, that theory is overdue for a reality check.

THE REAL FUNCTIONS OF GOVERNMENT

In the tradition of the classical political philosophy, Simon takes government to be natural and integral to human association. But he also contributes substantially to that tradition not only by his detailed analysis of the functions of political authority but also by showing how the proper exercise of those functions favors democratic government. Thus relegating references to classical texts to the footnotes, Simon begins his exposition with an example that commands general assent. Functions of political government may be a controversial subject, but everyone is more or less agreed on the nature and scope of parental authority. Before they can take care of themselves, children must be guided by their parents for their own good. Their own powers being undeveloped and inadequate, children depend on the experience, the reason, and the will of their parents, often enough for their physical survival as well as for their personal development. In this situation there is a deficiency, normal as it may be, and it indeed calls for government. Moreover, far from being considered a necessary evil, that government—parental care of children—is praised by all as unqualifiedly good. What Simon adds to this consensus is the reminder that even as exercised for the good of the governed, proper parental authority must remain substitutional and pedagogical. Parents fail their function if they do not teach their children to become independent.[32]

Political government, too, has a "parental" function in the exercise of which it compensates for what may be lacking in the individuals or collectives under its jurisdiction. This is the busiest function of any government, including democratic government. But since in democracy anything government does is bound to be criticized by someone, we need an example of the exercise of this "parental" function of political authority that should be acceptable to most. So instead of arguing about whether government should take care of orphans, or whether there are any limits to the federal encroachment on State rights, we turn to an enlightening example from American history. The victory in the Revolutionary War gave the American confederation extensive territories outside the boundaries of its original thirteen States. And so, in 1789, the Northwest Ordinance placed these territories under the government of the Union, which was both to govern the territories and to facilitate their development. In fact, the Ordinance stipulated that when the population of a given territory reached a certain number, that territory would be granted partial self-government, and when the number of its residents passed 50,000, that territory would became eligible to apply for statehood, "on an equal footing with the original states in all respects whatsoever." Thus thirty-six of the American States (Texas is the exception) were the wards, as it were, of the Union before they became its full-fledged and equal members.

In its ordinary exercise, this substitutional, "parental," function of government covers cases under provisions of both criminal and civil laws of every nation. But even as its actions benefit individual citizens, these actions are taken by the government on behalf of the community as a whole and for the sake of its common good. There should thus be no quarrel either about the need for this "parental" function of government, which does indeed spring from a great variety of deficiencies in the human condition, or about its purpose. Even the Jeffersonian best government, which is supposed to govern least, has the ultimate responsibility to act when something goes seriously wrong in society, due either to events in nature or to human action. This guarantees that government at all levels will keep busy all the time. But that does not mean that this, its most visible and enduring function, is also the only legitimate business of government, democratic government included.

To show that coping with deficiencies is not the only responsibility of political authority, Simon proposes that we consider a model of a perfect self-governing community. This community is free of deficiencies, because all its members are assumed to be both intelligent and well-intentioned; there is among them neither ignorance nor ill will that could cause authority to step in. Moreover, because this community is self-governing, we avoid confusing the need for government pure and simple with the related but different problem of the need for a distinct governing personnel. What Simon wants to know is how policy decisions are arrived at by such a community, and his first answer is surprisingly simple. This self-governing community of intelligent and well-intentioned people will make its decisions either by unanimity or by authority. There is no third way. Either all members agree on what should be done, or some must accept the others' decision. For instance, shall we drive on the right side of the road or on the left side? It may not matter which, but if we are not unanimous, we have to settle it, for the good of all as well as of each, by way of authority (which could well be the authority of chance invoked by flipping a coin). Big or small, all decisions pertaining to action affecting the whole community are subject to this condition.[33]

The next logical step is to estimate the chances this ideal self-governing community has of making policy by unanimity rather than by authority. Would intelligent and well-intentioned men and women tend to be unanimous about what has to be done, thus dispensing with the need to resort to authority? Simon divides his answer in two parts. If the action to be decided upon happens to be uniquely determined, they should indeed be unanimous. In such a case, that is, if there is no other way, any difference of opinion or reluctance to go along would be a sign either of a failure to understand what is at stake or of a failure of the will to act, both of which are excluded from the model by definition. But if, alternately, this self-governing community is presented with several equally sound options, no amount of intelligence or degree of civic virtue among its citizens-rulers can guarantee that they will be unanimous in choosing the same particular course of action. In this case, they must resort to authority in order to decide, say, by majority vote, the policy they will all follow. Unanimity is ruled out by the presence of genuine choices.

Simon's final argument illustrates nicely the thoroughness of his approach. Suppose we are presented with alternatives *a, b, c,* and *d.* With more information about these options and about the whole situation, should it not be possible for intelligent and well-intentioned citizens to pick the one that is demonstrably the best? Many modern social scientists seem to believe that social science should eventually be able to assure such selection, but that may well have more to do with their methodological bias than with their own empirical investigations. For why, indeed, should improved knowledge of all the factors involved in a given situation be expected to reduce all policy options, in all cases, to a single, demonstrably best solution? We expect breakthroughs in natural sciences to widen our choices, and there is no reason to expect less from progress in the social sciences. Knowledge is a kind of power, and all power points to freedom of choice rather than "beyond freedom."[34]

Eschewing technical arguments, Simon offers a simple but conclusive example. He invites us to consider the case of a family planning a vacation. If they are poor, ignorant of places to go, and in bad health to boot, their choices are clearly limited, if indeed they have a choice. Under those circumstances, they would probably have to stay at home, or, at best, impose on some relatives living in the country nearby. But if the family is rich, in excellent health, and familiar with all the nicest vacation spots in the whole world, their choices become practically infinite. But at the same time, of course, there is also far less chance that this family would unanimously decide where to go and, consequently, if they are to go anywhere together, they will have to choose by way of authority, be that of the father or the mother, or the wishes of the youngest child, or the majority of all the members.[35]

Other examples of this principle can be found at all levels of social experience. For instance, all other things being equal, an advanced nation has more options with regard to any number of policies than a so-called developing nation. This is so because destitution, ill health, weakness, uncertainty, ignorance—in a word, any and all deficiencies—restrict choice and cause dependence on specific means. By contrast, abundance, good health, assurance, achievement, power, and knowledge (including sound social science) are factors that clearly contribute to the widening of our choices. And that is how Simon is led to conclude that choosing among equally suitable courses of common action is indeed a necessary and essential function of political authority. Here, the need to resort to authority is due not on account of any deficiency but, on the contrary, it increases in proportion as deficiencies, including especially ignorance and ill will, are removed from the situation. Simon writes:

> The function of authority with which we are concerned, i.e., that of procuring united action when the means to the common good are several does not disappear but grows, as deficiencies are made up; it originates not in the defects of men and societies, but in the nature of society. It is an essential function.[36]

What needs perhaps to be added here is that, if political liberty is understood as superdetermined self-government, its true test becomes the ability to honor such legitimate decisions of political authority. In democracy, political liberty is involved both in the making of political decisions and in their implementation.[37]

LIBERTY AND AUTHORITY WORKING TOGETHER

For the supreme test of the complementariness of democratic liberty and authority, however, we must go beyond their necessary collaboration in deciding upon and implementing common action. Laws and policies are but means to the common good. The common good as an end must be intended and willed separately from and prior to the choosing of means by which it is to be realized. And this is indeed why this intending and willing of the common good of society, which in democracy depends on a corresponding exercise of political liberty, constitutes, according to Simon, the "most essential" function of political authority. Having established that realistically and strictly speaking the only place where the common good of a society can be found is in the minds and hearts of its members, that is also the place to look for the ultimate resolution of the potential conflict between liberty and authority.

To prepare the reader for the formal statement of his thesis, Simon offers a number of descriptive examples of which we may choose two. The first example is that of a small liberal arts college with the faculty doubling as its governing board. The advantage of this model is again twofold. It closely approximates a perfect self-governing community, in which the essence of authority is not obscured either by substitutional functions related to some deficiency, or by the problem of a distinct governing body. And it is also an example in which unity in diversity as a requirement of the common good is plainly visible and indisputable.

The faculty of this small liberal arts college is composed of a teacher of English, a teacher of Latin, a teacher of Philosophy, a teacher of History, and a teacher of Mathematics, all of whom are quite competent in their fields and exceptionally dedicated to their school. As such, they are all naturally strong individuals, but there is a particularly pronounced difference in the attitude of the Latin teacher and that of the teacher of Mathematics. The latter is a woman with great skills in interpersonal relations and an unblemished reputation for objectivity, which she enjoys. At faculty meetings, it is usually she who mediates between opposing views, while seldom saying anything that might sound like a promotion for mathematics. By contrast, of the Latin teacher they say that, if he had his way, he would convert every youngster into a Latin scholar, regardless of how ignorant his students might remain in mathematics, modern languages, or even Greek. The Latin teacher is the campus character, the subject of many good-natured jokes, but on occasion also a somewhat disrupting presence at the faculty board meetings. Indeed, watching his single-minded performances, one is tempted to call into question the genuineness of his dedication to the school's overall interests. But that, according to Simon, could be a mistake. For among this man's motives, a keen sense of service to society, as well as to the college, is not the least plausible. This old scholar's passionate attachment to his subject need not mean that he overdoes the importance of the classics and ignores that of mathematics. As Simon sees it, the attitude of this Latin teacher could well represent a true commitment to the good of society, which, all other things being equal, would be a better society, if a few people in it knew Vergil, than if Vergil was entirely unknown there. In other words, and contrary to superficial appearances, the common good of society rather than harmed is well served by individuals consciously and strongly dedicated to the promotion of particular goods.[38]

Simon's other example is taken from real life where regular authorities have to deal with every kind of human deficiencies. It is the case of a father tried for a serious crime. The man is guilty and the judge, in charge of upholding public order, will have to see to it that he is duly punished. But what about the wife of the criminal? She is innocent and happens to be a loyal, law-abiding citizen no less concerned about public order than the judge himself. Should she side with the court, or should she stand by her husband and the father of her children? Clearly, doing everything possible to have her husband back in the family, she goes contrary to what the good of the society demands. Does that make her a bad citizen and a bad person? Most people would say, No, for one reason or another. Simon does too, but for a special reason. Standing by her husband, he explains, the wife is doing the right thing, because that is exactly what the common good of society demands. Formally, she is in compliance with the common good; her material opposition to it springs from the plurality, diversity, and contingency in human life. The common good demands that persons in charge of particular goods attend to those goods (in her case, her family). "That particular goods be properly defended by particular persons," Simon writes, "matters greatly for the common good itself." Taking care of the common good both formally and materially considered, namely, seeing to it that justice is done and that this particular man is punished, is up to the judge representing the government of the community.[39]

What these examples indicate is that for the good of the political community, *both* particular goods *and* the common good must be specifically intended and promoted, which can only be done by authority and liberty working together. But before citing Simon's formal statement of this requirement, it may help to take a quick look at two familiar American Constitutional arrangements which also exemplify it. The first is the Presidential Cabinet, the second the American federalism. When the President meets with his Cabinet to consider and formulate his administration's overall program, what exactly is he supposed to do? Ideally, he will listen carefully to the proposals by the heads of the various departments; he will mediate the inevitable conflict between departmental interests; and he will trim, balance, and coordinate these proposals into what to him seems to be the best overall fit. To do that, he will of course need the best possible input from every department secretary, who should offer it in a free, uninhibited, even passionate manner. But what everybody takes for granted and tends therefore to ignore is the one prior and absolutely essential requirement for the President to do his job properly. Before he even begins to listen to the members of his Cabinet, and continuously throughout his interaction with them leading to his final decisions, what the President has to have on his mind and wish for in his heart is what is best for the United States. That is what both the people and the Constitution as well as his department secretaries expect will guide his specific final decisions. Translated in Simon's terms, this expectation reveals the President's most essential function: to *intend* and *will* the nation's common good both *materially* and *formally* considered.

The federal division of sovereignty under the Constitution of the United States, a perennial topic of debates on American constitutional law and politics, can also be intelligently explained as not so much a division of power as the division of labor between liberty and authority in the intending and willing the fullness of the nation's common good. Indeed, the political system invented at Philadelphia may be said to embody this principle writ large. The Constitution puts the government of the Union in full charge of the overall common good of the United States, and charges the States to take care of their own particular common goods. Formally loyal to the Union, the States are at liberty to pursue their own common goods materially considered. The Constitution, in other words, grants the states the inalienable rights to "life, liberty, and the pursuit of happiness," and charges the Union, among other things, to "secure these rights." In the federal arrangement of *e pluribus unum*, the so-called state sovereignty is political liberty writ large under the political authority of the Union affirmed in the supremacy clause of the Constitution. As Chief Justice Chase wrote in *Texas v. White* (1869), "The Constitution, in all its provisions, looks to an indestructible Union, composed of indestructible States." But what we need also to recognize in the present context is what may be called the true dynamics of the federal arrangement. Nothing in this arrangement prevents the federal and the State governments from improving the performance of their constitutionally assigned functions at the same time. Under federalism there is no need for any trade-offs between liberty and authority. The government of the Union and the governments of the States, the former representing Authority, the latter Liberty, can well grow together to produce an ever more perfect union. The ideal democratic polity, then, may be seen as a sort of federal union writ small. Its common good is fulfilled jointly by the individual citizens exercising their civil rights and the government performing its essential function.

Simon's more formal statement of what he calls the most essential function of political authority is as follows. While civic virtue (true liberty) includes the willingness to subordinate one's own interests to the good of society, the good of society may be intended formally without being intended materially. Civic virtue (true liberty) guarantees the intention of the common good formally considered, *not* the intention of the common good materially considered. In fact, society would be harmed if everyone were to intend the common good not only formally but also materially, precisely because particular goods would then be neglected. In their private capacity, citizens ought to intend particular goods, which in democracy is their right and constitutes both their formal and material liberty. But under this arrangement, the political authority, representing public reason and public will, however institutionally constituted, must assume the ultimate and essential responsibility for the intending and willing the common good both materially and formally considered.[40]

Beyond the distraction of ideological arguments and daily politics, Simon here lets us see that the pursuit of genuine common good of society requires joint exercise of political authority and political liberty. It is a pity that Hannah Arendt overlooked Simon's contribution when she complained that we no longer understand the idea of freedom, because "practically as well as theoretically, we no longer . . . know what authority *is*."[41] Simon brings political freedom and political authority together for all to understand: "What we find at the core of the most essential function of authority," he writes in conclusion to his exposition, "is that autonomy renders authority necessary and authority renders autonomy possible."[42] It is a finding that restores realism to political theorizing. And Mortimer Adler, for one, did not miss its implication for the theory of democracy. Citing Simon's exposition, he put it as follows: "We can see here that the existence of political liberty is indispensable to a government's having an essential, and not merely a substitutional, authority; for essential authority inheres only in the laws or institutions of a self-governing people."[43]

American democratic culture is saturated with suspicion of all authority, and Simon is aware that his interpretation is bound to be criticized.[44] But for Simon, firmness of convictions about authority as well as liberty is an indispensable requirement for a viable democracy, which is in constant need of reaffirmation, precisely because a democratic society is forever tempted by a kind of political hedonism. With a glance at the historical record, Simon writes:

All too often the hard exigencies of democratic action were concealed by the association of democratic rhetoric with hedonistic philosophy. Politicians and theorists, all hungry for cheap popularity, spread the belief that democracy exacts little, welcomes soft characters, keeps citizens from heroic enterprises, lessens pain and exertion, shuns dreams of grandeur, and prefers the easy way.[45]

One has to admit that this describes fairly at least the daily surface of the opinions and contemparary attitudes of many people. Even though most American citizens believe in the basic *truths* embodied in the Declaration of Independence and the Constitution, they also like to pretend that democracy is a kind of system that can take care of itself.[46] This democratic faith, as it is sometimes called, lumps democratic government together with the principle of liberty, equality, universal suffrage, the consent of the governed and majority rule, as if they all naturally and spontaneously always agree with each other. And if they happen to clash, the remedy recommended is often simply more democracy. Simon takes democracy more seriously. And he gladly trades popular appeal for truth and realistic practical recommendations.

NOTES

1. Isaiah Berlin, "Two Concepts of Liberty," in *Four Essays on Liberty* (New York: Oxford University Press, 1969).

2. See *The Idea of Freedom: Essays in Honour of Isaiah Berlin*, ed. Alan Ryan (New York: Oxford University Press, 1979). The collection includes essays by Charles Taylor, Stuart Hampshire, and Bernard Williams, all of whom praise Berlin's contribution but also take exception to some of his theses.

3. Mortimer J. Adler, *The Idea of Freedom*, 2 vols. (Garden City, NY: Doubleday and Company, 1958, 1961), Parts III and IV.

4. Simon mentions Berlin's *The Hedgehog and the Fox* in *Practical Knowledge*, ed. Robert J. Mulvaney (New York: Fordham University Press, 1991), p. 38n5.

5. *The Idea of Freedom*, p. 592.

6. *The Spirit of Laws*, ed. David Wallace Carriters (Berkeley, CA: University of California Press), pp. xi, 3.

7. Yves R. Simon, *Freedom of Choice*, ed. Peter Wolf (New York: Fordham University Press, 1969, 1987), p. 157.

8. Ibid., p. 2.

9. A. S. Eddington, *The Nature of the Physical World* (New York: Macmillan,

1927), p. 350; quoted in Simon, *Freedom of Choice* (New York: Fordham University Press, 1969), p. 14.

10. *Freedom of Choice*, p. 153.

11. See *The Liberalism-Communitarianism Debate*, ed. C. F. Delaney (Lanham, MD: Rowman and Littlefield, 1994); *Rights and the Common Good: The Communitarian Perspective*, ed. Amitai Etzioni (New York: St. Martin's Press, 1995); and *Catholicism, Liberalism, and Communitarianism*, ed. K. L. Grasso, G. V. Bradley, and R. B. Hunt (Lanham, MD: Rowman and Littlefield, 1995). See also Michael Sandel, *Democracy's Discontent: America in Search of Public Philosophy* (Cambridge, MA: The Belknap Press of the Harvard University Press, 1996), and Stephen Holmes, *The Anatomy of Antiliberalism* (Cambridge, MA: Harvard University Press, 1993).

12. The 1995 annual publication of the American Maritain Association, *Freedom, Virtue, and the Common Good*, edited by Curtis L. Hancock and Anthony O. Simon (Notre Dame, IN: Notre Dame University Press, 1995), includes five chapters by different contributors discussing Simon's interpretation of these subjects.

13. Friedrich Nietzsche, *The Birth of Tragedy* (Garden City, NY: Doubleday Anchor Books, 1956), p. 24.

14. *Natural Law*, p. 93

15. Friedrich A. Hayek, *The Constitution of Liberty* (Chicago, IL: University of Chicago Press, 1960), p. 144. See also Robert Nozik, *Anarchy, State, and Utopia* (New York: The Viking Press, 1974), p. 39.

16. Yves R. Simon, *The Tradition of Natural Law* (New York: Fordham University Press, 1965, 1992), p. 106; from Harold Laski, *Liberty in the Modern State* (New York: The Viking Press, 1949), p. 39.

17. Ibid., p. 107.

18. Robert A. Dahl, *Democracy and Its Critics* (New Haven, CT: Yale University Press, 1989), pp. 72, 218.

19. A generation ago, Glendon A. Schubert urged political scientists to devote their time and effort to "nurturing more useful concepts," becaue the notion of public interest made no "operational sense." *The Public Interest: A Critique of the Theory of a Political Concept* (Glenco, IL: Free Press, 1960), p. 224.

20. See Simon, *Material Logic*, Part II, "On the Universal," and Part IV, Question 17, "On Relation."

21. A dozen years before the publication of Rawls's *Theory of Justice*, and echoing the famous declaration by Wilhelm von Humboldt, which John Stuart Mill used as the motto for his *On Liberty*, Christian Bay wrote as follows: "The maximization of every man's and woman's freedom—psychological, social, and potential—is the only proper first-priority for the joint human effort that we call political." Christian Bay, *The Structure of Freedom* (Stanford, CA: Stanford University Press, 1958), p. 390.

22. See Vukan Kuic, "Federalism as a Model of Political Association," in *Politics 72: Trends in Federalism*, ed. Tinsley E. Yarbrough et al. (Greenville, NC: East Carolina University Publications, 1972), pp. 5–20.

23. *Natural Law*, p. 91.

24. Stephen Holmes denies that the liberals subordinate the public to the private realm, and attributes this widely held impression to political tactics liberals had to use in their historical struggle for individual rights. *The Anatomy of Antiliberalism*, ch. 12, "The Public Realm Sacrificed to the Private?"

25. *Politics 3.4.1277ᵇ7–15*. The relevant statement is that the good citizen should know how to govern like a freeman and to obey like a freeman.

26. *Natural Law*, p. 98.

27. Quoted in *The Anatomy of Antiliberalism*, p. 198. Stephen Holmes affirms that liberals have never abandoned common good as legal standard.

28. Friedrich Engels, *Socialism: Utopian and Scientific*, in *Marx and Engels: Basic Writings on Politics and Philosophy*, ed. Lewis S. Feuer (New York: Doubleday 1959), p. 106.

29. *Common Sense*, in *The Writings of Thomas Paine* (New York: G. P. Putnam's Sons, 1894), vol. 1, p. 69.

30. *The Federalist* No. 51 (Modern Library edition), p. 337.

31. Yves R. Simon, *Philosophy of Democratic Government* (Chicago: University of Chicago Press, 1951), pp. 1–7.

32. Ibid., pp. 7–19.

33. *Democratic Government*, pp. 19–35; *General Theory of Authority* (Notre Dame, IN: University of Notre Dame Press, 1962, 1980), pp. 47–50.

34. Simon comments as follows: "When psychologists do not altogether deny freedom of choice, they generally trace it to an imperfection or uncertainty of the will, to an element of looseness in its operation. Similarly, many social thinkers, when confronted by a seeming plurality of means, trace it to inadequate knowledge and fail to see that plurality of genuine means can be caused by excellence of knowledge and power. In both cases the misunderstanding results from an insufficiently elaborate notion of causality." *Democratic Government*, p. 35.

35. Ibid., pp. 32–33.

36. Ibid., p. 33.

37. There is no difference here between the communitarian and the liberal positions. For as Stephen Holmes puts it, "liberal citizens are obliged to follow the law because, they, as a collectivity, imposed it on themselves and retain the power to change it." *The Anatomy of Antiliberalism*, p. 229.

38. *Democratic Government*, pp. 45–46.

39. Ibid., p. 41.

40. Ibid., p. 48.

41. Hannah Arendt, *Between Past and Future* (New York: Meridian Books, 1963), p. 92.

42. *Democratic Government*, p. 71.

43. Adler, *The Idea of Freedom*, vol. 1, p. 345.

44. "Why is it," Simon asks, "that men distrust so intensely a thing [authority] without which they cannot, by all evidence, live and act together?" His answer is that authority often appears in conflict with the greater good not only of liberty but also of justice, truth, and order. Consequently, a philosopher wanting to discuss authority objectively must be prepared to meet with "suspicion and malice." *General Theory of Authority*, p. 13. This Simon's question is taken by Eugene Kennedy and Sara C. Charles for the motto of their recent book *Authority: The Most Misunderstood Idea in America* (New York: Free Press, 1997).

45. *Democratic Government*, p. 17.

46. See Michael Kammen, *Machine That Would Go of Itself: The Constitution in American Culture* (New York: Knopf, 1986).

4

CONSTITUTIONAL DEMOCRACY

D emocracy, Simon tells us, belongs to the class of regimes in which the resistance of the people to bad government as well as overgovernment is institutionally organized and which, therefore, deserve to be called "political." Simon calls the other type of regimes "despotic," but he is careful to point out that even such a regime may sometimes do the right thing. For instance, few would think that Catherine the Great did wrong when she ordered that the peasants be vaccinated against smallpox against their will.[1] Over time and in different places, the institutional, political resistance to arbitrary rule has been organized in various ways. In the European experience, before the rise of democracy, the customary privileges of aristocracies had not infrequently restrained gross abuse of royal power, which is one reason why *Magna Carta* is still considered a symbol of liberty. Quoting Lord Acton, Simon also suggests that because under the canon law the autonomy of the inferior ranks is as well protected as the authority of the superior ranks, even the organization of the Catholic Church can be termed "political."[2] Democracy, however, institutionalizes resistance against abuse of governmental powers in the most radical way. Rather than soliciting charters of liberty from sovereign rulers, or relying on mutual recognition of status, democracy establishes the people themselves as the exclusive source of all power of government. Madison called it an "unmixed republic," but one can hardly improve on his definition of what is today called democracy. It is "a government which derives *all* its powers directly or indirectly from the great body of the people, and is administered by persons holding their offices during pleasure, for a limited period, or during good behavior."[3] Still, to make this definition fit better the current understanding of democratic politics, it helps to state explicitly the latent ambition behind it. The people in democracy want more than just to protect their rights and liberties. What they want is *to govern* themselves. "Every democracy," Simon writes, "remains, in varying degrees, a direct democracy."[4]

This sense of popular government is incorporated in such practices as initiative, recall, and referendum, in addition to the more common periodic elections. Less formal arrangements by means of which the people in a democracy retain their original sovereignty are found in the contacts the constituents maintain with their representatives between elections and, of course, in the attention public officials pay to Public Opinion. But the basic principles under which modern representative democracies assert popular sovereignty and carry on the government "by the people" are clearly the following: the consent of the governed, universal suffrage, and majority rule. Democratic constitutional debates at the highest level are mostly about the meaning and the proper application of these principles. Simon's realistic interpretation compares well with the rest.

POPULAR SOVEREIGNTY AND THE CONSENT OF THE GOVERNED

Prior to the rise of modern politics, Simon recalls, sovereignty, i.e., the power to bind a person's conscience, was routinely traced to divine authority.[5] According to some of those old interpretations, this sovereign power was given by God directly to the kings, who then ruled in his name. But other "divine right" theories held, on the contrary, that the original recipient of sovereignty were the people, who then duly transmitted it to the kings. In fact, this "transmission theory" even allowed the people, under certain circumstances, to take back their sovereignty. Thus Francisco Suarez, for one, held that direct democracy was the natural, divinely ordained human condition, from which all other forms of political association are derived by man-made provisions.[6] Contrary to the prevailing opinions, then, "divine right" theories are not all the same, and Simon notes that the "transmission theory," which places sovereignty originally in the people, is compatible with the conventional understanding of how modern representative democracy works.

There is, nevertheless, a decisive difference between the old and the new theories of popular sovereignty, and this difference points to the main source of the confusion and problems in interpreting the power of "binding consciences" in modern democracy. The medieval doctrine designates the community as such as its collective earthly possessor. But the modern theory pushes the origin of sovereignty beyond a "social contract" to locate it in effect in its individual signatories. This is what the models offered by Hobbes, Locke, and Rousseau have in common. They may give different specific reasons why their solitary sovereign individuals contract with each other, and they differ on the specific provisions of their imaginary social contracts. But regardless of the conditions Hobbes, Locke, and Rousseau assume to prevail in the state of nature, and regardless of the difference in the arrangements they propose for the state of civil society, all their social contracts are inspired by acknowledged selfish interests of the contracting individuals. In a nutshell, that interest is, for Hobbes, sheer survival, for Locke, convenience, and for Rousseau, equality. It is in order to secure these personal benefits, unavailable in "the state of nature," described as insecure, inconvenient, and unequal, that their "free" individuals contract to transfer their original sovereignty, and freedom, to a civil society empowered to bind consciences. Under Hobbes's *Leviathan*, the transfer is absolute, and its subjects have no say in the government. Rousseau in a sense wants to have it both ways, but in the end he empowers the governing General Will to "force" citizens "to be free." And while Locke also acknowledges the contractual transfer of sovereignty as binding, his contract carries over the individuals' "natural rights" into the construction of civil society, where they become qualified civil rights. Today, none of these theories is taken seriously. But that does not mean that the "sovereign individual" does not still figure in modern political speculations.

For instance, even though his ideally just democratic society is established blindly and fairly by the consent of all, John Rawls still insists that everyone must retain forever the right to civil disobedience. Why? Precisely because Rawls's free and unencumbered individuals sign his social contract exclusively out of self-interest. They do not want to take any chances. And Rawls's "difference principle" makes here no difference. The principle of favoring the least advantaged is acceptable to all precisely because they could be its beneficiaries. Behind the veil of ignorance, they are taking out insurance against landing at the bottom of the social pile. Yet Rawls refuses to make any commitment absolutely binding. He writes:

> In a democratic society, then, it is recognized that each citizen is responsible for his interpretation of the principles of justice and for his conduct in the light of them. There can be no legally or socially approved rendering of these principles that we are always morally bound to accept, not even when it is given by a supreme court or legislature.
> . . . The final court of appeal is not the court, nor the executive, nor the legislature, but the electorate as a whole. The civilly disobedient appeal in a special way to this body.[7]

As Simon explains it, the institutionalized resistance against bad government and overgovernment in democracy includes the understanding that democratic citizens never let sovereignty completely out of their hands. But no matter how much resistance it may allow, democratic government clearly must also have compliance, both in practice and in theory. Yet Rawls nowhere even considers any possible morally obligatory grounds for civil *obedience* in democracy. Suppose the "electorate as a whole" (nominally representing popular sovereignty but reduced in practice to the majority of the voters) turns down the appeal of Rawls's "civilly disobedient" democrats who brought their case before it. For those citizens to decide then whether to obey or not, would it not help to know *why*? Hobbes, Locke, and Rousseau all combine practical necessity with formal contractual commitment to acknowledge the individuals' obligations in civil society. In their widely different ways, they all nevertheless affirm that in order to secure the advantages of life in common, certain rules must be obeyed for the good of all. And if that is so, it clearly follows that individuals have a certain *moral obligation* to obey those rules.[8] Burdened with the assumption of some original sovereignty possessed by individuals, rather than by the community, Rawls is reluctant to acknowledge any such obligation.

And he is not alone. Because the United States Constitution has not protected the interests of all American citizens equally, Sanford Levinson recently wrote that he would not blame the members of the groups that have been shortchanged in the distribution of its benefits, if they renounced "faith" in the Constitution and concluded that the document is not binding upon them. As "a white, male, well-paid law professor," however, he has less personal reasons not to "sign up" to the Constitution, and in fact he is inclined to do so. But in what appears as a rather dubious identification with those less privileged, Levinson will do it only with a very specific reservation. He writes:

> [W]hat makes my faith assertion only a limited one is the recognition that even my "best" Constitution might at times come into conflict with what I regard as my most important moral commitments; under such circumstances, it would be the Constitution that (I hope) would give way.[9]

In one sense, Levinson could be said to reserve for himself the right to refuse ever to be "forced to be free." But his explicit elevation of unspecified personal "moral values" over an equally personal interpretation of the Consitution (which, incidentally, he defines as but "a linguistic system") reveals a peculiar understanding of the consent of the governed in democracy. What Levinson denies, more explicitly than Rawls, is that individual citizens in a democracy can ever be *morally* bound by the "legally and socially approved rendering of the principles of justice." And while saying so may be currently fashionable among some contemporary theorists of democracy (as well as among members of various citizens' militias), one has to question whether this position makes much sense, either practical or theoretical. Every democracy may be a direct democracy in some sense, but a democratic government simply cannot work, if what sovereignty is transferred to it by the people remains forever revocable at the discretion of individual citizens who happen to find a particular policy duly decided by that government in conflict with their personal "moral" values. The ideal of the *government* of the people, for the people, and by the people cannot even be explained, let alone practiced, if democratic citizens, whether privileged or underprivileged, collectively or individually, reserve for themselves the right to interpret their consent at will.

But let it also be noted that submitting every political disagreement to the electorate at large, in the name of popular sovereignty, would also be rather counterproductive. Regarding this issue, Madison's reply to Jefferson is definitive. Besides stirring up emotions and disrupting the normal political and governmental processes, such appeals would do no good, Madison writes, because they too would be decided by partisan majorities, since "a nation of philosophers is as little to be expected as the philosophical race of kings wished for by Plato."[10] And if one plebiscite is decided on partisan grounds, others are bound to follow, assuring that the "civilly disobedient" will never cease out of the land.

But Rawls's and Levinson's positions are not only impractical. They also contradict any number of ethical–political theories, including the old *pacta sunt servanda* no less than Kant's categorical imperative. Their propositions cannot be willed without contradiction to become the universal rule of personal conduct. Civil disobedience may not be a contradiction in terms, but neither is its meaning, as opposed to possible practice, entirely at the personal discretion of individuals. The right thing to do, the true free choice of any mature, self-governing individual citizen living under any political regime as defined above, and *before* making use of the institutions provided to stake any claims to civil disobedience, is first of all to acknowledge the binding power of just laws and lawful authority. Democracy is no exception to this rule. The institutionalized resistance to bad government or overgovernment in democracy does not include an a priori right of individual citizens to renege on the "social contract" established by the consent of all as the foundation of the democratic polity. In fact, *civil disobedience* makes sense only if it is assumed that duly enacted democratic laws do have the power to bind one's conscience. For what else can Rawls's "civilly disobedient" hope for, when appealing to "the electorate as a whole" (against Congress, the President, and the Supreme Court) except to have their claims vindicated by laws having such power? In democracy, the decision by the majority of the electorate marks the transition from politics to government. When chosen among other candidates, a Presidential candidate becomes the President of the United States. Claiming the right to disobedience *on principle* belongs more under a despotic than a democratic regime.

Rawls's and Levinson's interpretations of democratic sovereignty and the consent of the governed go against common sense and are easily disproved by experience. A viable democracy cannot do without mandatory observance of its charters, compacts, and bills of rights. The obligation to honor the Constitution is included in the meaning not only of the consent of the governed but also that of personal self-government. The champions of the priority of individual rights tend to minimize, if not to overlook completely, the indispensable communal context in which alone civil rights, including that of dissent, can be secured. It is as if they want to enjoy the benefits of civil society while claiming at the same time the alleged freedoms of an imaginary state of nature. Thus even as spirited a defender of liberalism as Stephen Holmes feels bound to admit that this is something contemporary liberal theory needs to address and to correct. "Statelessness," he explains, means "rightlessness." No matter how weary we may be of likely abuse and expansion of government, we must recognize that govermental power is as much enabling as it is restrictive.[11] The plain truth of the matter is that, if they really care to enjoy their rights, citizens in democracy cannot appeal just to the Bill of Rights; they must also support the Constitution.

Simon considers the requirement of the consent of the governed affirming the principle of popular sovereignty a glorious and irreversible historical achievement. Other political regimes may also rely on the consent of the governed, but what distinguishes democratic practice is precisely its radical dependence on the free consent by individual citizens. Rawls is exactly right when he says that, in democratic society, each citizen is uniquely responsible for his or her conduct in the light of his or her interpretation of the principles of justice. Democratic citizens are indeed supposed to make up their own minds about what they owe each other. But it hardly follows from this that the democratic, legal, and social rendering of principles of justice carries no moral obligation, does not in any way bind the conscience of the individual citizen. Democratic government expressing the will of the majority of the citizens is, of course, neither infallible nor incapable of committing injustice. But to claim, therefore, for each individual citizen a permanent discretionary right to civil disobedience, while ignoring any obligation to obey, seems hardly conducive to the formation of that overlapping consensus which Rawls recommends as the salvation of democracy.

Taking a broader historical-theoretical overview of the theory and practice of popular sovereignty and of government by the consent of the governed, Simon suggests the following interpretation. The principle of the consent of the governed may refer to and express (a) an essential condition of all *lawful* government—as opposed to any sort of usurpation of power; (b) a condition proper to *political* government, that is, the type that provides for institutionalized resistance to overgovernment and bad government; and (c) some condition proper to *democratic* government, that is, one subject to regular elections, initiative, recall, plebiscite, etc. Together, these meanings define democracy as a lawful political government embodying the principle of popular sovereignty and individual rights. But if the meaning of the consent of the governed is reduced to the claim that in a democracy "the governed are never bound except by their own consent—that they never have to obey except inasmuch as they please to obey," the principle, Simon holds, expresses "neither a political nor a democratic necessity but mere revolt against the laws of all community."[12]

UNIVERSAL SUFFRAGE

Early modern liberal theorists, including John Stuart Mill, saw nothing wrong with restricting franchise to men of property and education. In our time, however, the demand for universal suffrage has become so pervasive that even the totalitarian regimes make a special show of having it. Simon welcomes this development as a historic victory for "the democracy of the common people." In democracy, all are entitled to a say in what pertains to public affairs, and any exclusion or discrimination is by definition undemocratic. But even as he affirms the absolute democratic rightness of the principle of universal suffrage, Simon cautions against expecting too much from its practice. Simon is concerned that naively optimistic views of its benefits may cause disappointment and detract from the real political achievement that the inclusion of the common people in politics represents.

According to Simon, the main practical advantage of universal suffrage is that the voters, even though less than paragons of morality themselves, may be expected, all other things being equal, not to choose the worst among the candidates available. Madison apparently had something like this in mind when he argued that inferior candidates have less chance to be chosen in large voting districts.[13] But Simon does not want us to overlook possible negative political influence of universal suffrage, and especially warns against confusing the voters with "the people," which tends to elevate electoral results to be presented as the ultimate (popularly approved) standards of right and wrong.[14] However muffled, Rawls's democratic "overlapping consensus" trumping all independent search for truths, and Rorty's insistence on the priority of democracy over philosophy, may be seen as examples of this democratic tendency. They also represent a romantic view of universal suffrage, which in fact

detracts from its democratic utility. Echoing the early democratic denun-
ciation of the corrupt lifestyles of the old aristocracies (and the eighteenth-century myths of the noble savage), this romatic view endows
the so-called lower classes of society with some sort of superior wisdom.
But modern history, Simon points out, has shown conclusively that expecting universal suffrage "to liberate all the treasures of humanity—
kindness, sound instincts, etc.—contained in the thick mass of the unso-
phisticated people" can lead to disappointment and cause bitter rejection
of democracy.[15]

Preserving the principle of universal suffrage and making it work for
democracy requires, then, that its practice be understood and interpreted
realistically. For instance, the purpose of giving everyone a vote should
not be seen as intended to get rid of "elitism" in politics. There is nothing undemocratic in electing people to positions of leadership who are
distinguished by education, expertise, various talents, strength of character, and even wealth. On the contrary, the dearth among people in
charge of talents, entrepreneurial spirit, dedication to public service, and
higher education would clearly reduce the quality of democratic government and life. In the nature of things human, excellence is not found
in numbers, and democratic voters should elect special people to be their
leaders. The true value of universal suffrage consists in keeping these
leaders responsible. And Simon wants us to recognize that abusing political power for personal gain is not the only way in which power corrupts.
Members of governing elites, the intellectuals no less than the idle rich,
are sometimes tempted to indulge their fancy in proposing unworkable
plans for the "construction of social reality." Possessed of universal suffrage as well as of "occupational guaranties of loyalty to the real," Simon
writes, it is the common people who are likely to keep politics down to
earth.[16]

What universal suffrage guarantees, then, is that even people "de-
void of the qualities sanctioned by definite social distinctions [must] not
be [left] constitutionally helpless."[17] Early in the twentieth century it was
still possible for a president of an American railroad company solemnly
and publicly to declare that "the rights and interests of the laboring man
will be protected and cared for, not by the labor agitators, but by the
Christian men to whom God in His infinite wisdom, has given control
of the property interests of the country."[18] The time, Simon contends,
when it was possible to hold that the destiny of the common people can

be safely entrusted to the wisdom of the upper classes is gone forever. The irreversible extension of voting rights has promoted and consolidated democratic liberties and equality, and additional gains can be expected from improving electoral laws and practices. But that certainly does not mean that all problems of democratic government are solved by giving everyone a vote.

MAJORITY RULE

With his European background, and writing only a few years after the end of the Second World War, it is not surprising that Simon would consider the problem of majority rule with reference to the failure of the democratic experiment in the Weimar Republic. Ever since Tocqueville, who raised it as a possibility, the threat of the "tyranny of the majority" has been duly acknowledged in modern political literature. But democracy with universal suffrage is equally exposed to the opposite danger, namely, the inability to produce any kind of majority, and the Weimar Republic is a case in point. As if to show how completely they have broken with their authoritarian past, the Germans in 1919 adopted for their brand new republic the electoral system of proportional representation, then hailed by some political theorists as a great democratic leap forward. As it happened, however, successive elections under this system quickly produced a large number of political parties, unstable coalition governments, confusion, loss of the initial enthusiasm for democracy, and led finally to Hitler.[19] But how did people get the idea in the first place that proportional representation is the epitome of democratic politics? Simon believes that the inspiration behind it is the illusory wish for government by unanimity. To be truly democratic, that is, literally of, for, and by the people, some seem to think that democratic government must include representatives from every social interest in the community. But this view confuses political representation with political authority, which are not the same even in democratic theory, let alone practice. While democracy indeed requires fair representation of the plurality of interests in society, it also needs its government to speak and act in unison. Thus while democratic political parties may be entitled to representation in the deliberative assembly in proportion to the number of votes they receive in an election, they cannot all have a proportionate share in the operation of the executive branch as well. In the real world, democratic government does not mean government by all; it means government by the majority.[20]

Proportional representation, then, is of no particular benefit to democracy and might even sabotage its proper operation under the required principle of majority rule. But if that is the potential effect of this apparently democratic principle pushed to the extreme, Simon wants next to consider whether a democratic regime may not benefit from including in its constitution some institutional arrangements and practices that do not embody the principle of majority rule. With a hint at the classical arguments in favor of mixed regimes, Simon is convinced that this is indeed the case. In order to avoid degenerating into anarchy, at one extreme, or stiffening into tyranny, at the other extreme, democracy, in his opinion, cannot put all its trust in the bare principle of majority rule. The best regime, Simon argues, cannot be any *simple* regime. Quoting both Aristotle and Aquinas, Simon agrees that the best regime is one in which several forms are "combined in such a way as to promote various aspects of the common good to each of which each political form is related in a special fashion." But the association of democracy with some nondemocratic principles may also protect democracy from some enemies from the inside.[21]

Simon does not elaborate on the American case, but the example is clearly relevant in discussion of constitutional democracy. What the American Founders saw in history of the Greek and the Italian experiments with democracy was their "perpetual vibrations between the extremes of tyranny and anarchy," the "pleasing scenes" of their life all too soon "overwhelmed by the tempestuous waves of sedition and party rage."[22] Set to establish popular government again on an unprecedented scale, the American Framers understood their task to be not only to devise a means to check the propensity of popular government to succumb to the violence of factions, of the majority as well as of the minorities; they also hoped thereby to rescue its reputation "from the opprobrium of mankind." Today, democracy is popular throughout the world, due not least to the historical success of the United States. But what is the secret, as it were, of the American Constitution that has enabled it to progress, slowly but surely, toward ever more inclusive democracy?[23]

According to Madison, the democratic (republican) ideals are well served by the "auxiliary precaution" of the separation of powers.[24] Now in our time, especially this feature of the Constitution has often been criticized for violating the principle of majority rule and producing a "deadlock of democracy."[25] But the fact is that, unlike the short-lived first French Republic, and the improved Weimar Republic, the United States has for two hundred years avoided both anarchy and the tyranny of the majority while becoming at the same time ever more democratic. And since the same Constitution is still in place, its provisions cannot be denied all credit for this development. In fact, despite all their criticism, not even the most radical upholders of democratic majority rule want to get rid of all checks upon it. Especially fond of the Bill of Rights, they conveniently overlook that its implementation depends directly on the principle of the separation of powers remaining in force. To remain true to its promise of life, liberty, and justice for all, democracy clearly can use, as Simon recommends, some nondemocratic constitutional aids.

DEMOCRATIC PLURALISM

The historical failure of the original French democratic revolution, whose ideals of liberty, equality, and fraternity he makes his own, is for Simon the prime example from which to draw practical lessons on how true democratic government, and individual liberties it is supposed to guarantee, may be spared such a fate. The absolutism of the French kings was defended by Bossuet on the grounds that "without this absolute authority, the king can neither do good, nor curb the evil; his power must be such that nobody may hope to escape it; and the only safeguard of particular persons against public power, must be their innocence."[26] Bossuet's argument did not prevent the Revolution in the name of liberty and equality, but its rationale was quickly adopted and applied with vengeance by the first modern version of a "people's republic." The new democracy was to be like the good king of Bossuet, to be trusted with the scope and the means of action which could not be safely put in any other hands. Simon calls this ideological sleight of hand the illusion of the democratic transformation of the state. And in his opinion, no amount of institutional "auxiliary precautions" is alone sufficient to prevent it from destroying a working democracy. Simon writes:

> The illusion of the democratic transformation of the state is completely dissipated when it is understood that, in order to save society

from state absolutism, it is not enough to incorporate into the structure of the state a system of checks, balances, and constitutional guarantees. Not even the ultimate check constituted by the control of the people over the governing personnel suffices; this control may not be genuine and it may also become the accomplice of state absolutism, for the passions which make for absolutism may get hold of the people itself, even though to its disadvantage. In democracy as well as in nondemocratic polities, the absolutism of the state must be held in check by forces external to the state apparatus. This does not mean that the guarantees procured by democratic forms are held ineffective or unimportant; they are important but would soon disappear if they were not supplemented by external institutions.[27]

Simon's list of these external institutions is the conventional one: free church, free press, independent universities, autonomous co-operatives, free labor unions, private property, and free enterprise. "The survival of democracy," he writes, "depends upon a *pluralistic* concept of social life, in which irreducible diversities, enduring antinomies, and difficult processes of adjustment or restoration play a considerable role."[28] Simon does not cite Madison's famous lines explaining why democracy has to put up, within generous limits, with social conflict, but that is what he has in mind. "Liberty is to faction," Madison writes,

what air is to fire, an aliment without which it instantly expires. But it could not be less folly to abolish liberty, which is essential to political life, because it nourishes faction, than it would be to wish the annihilation of air, which is essential to animal life, because it imparts to fire its destructive agency.[29]

Thus despite the damage that, for instance, labor disorders may cause, Simon is adamant that, if the right to strike is abolished, "liberty is gone and death is coming."[30] In democratic constitutional practice, factionalism must be accepted as an unavoidable feature of social diversity. But social pluralism and the right of dissent, according to Simon, keep democracy alive also in another more profound sense.

We tend to think of civil rights primarily as "negative" individual rights that protect citizens against what those in power might want to do to them. Upon reflection, however, we begin to realize that the politically most important democratic rights are in fact both positive and collective. This is so not just because these rights are supposed to be enjoyed by everyone, but rather because their actual exercise always involves more than single isolated individuals. Freedom of assembly is the obvious example, and we should not be misled by the *language* of the First Amendment to classify it as "negative."[31] It is the same with the freedom of religion, press, and speech, for it is only the active believers, readers, and audiences that can give these freedoms political meaning. Moreover, even those "negative rights" offering protection to individuals, say, against double jeopardy, or cruel and unusual punishment, depend in turn on support from a free press, free political parties, and free speech. The guarantee of individual civil rights is thus not the ultimate purpose of a democratic constitution. That guarantee is part of its overall institutional structure which provides for resistance to bad government and over-government and thus qualifies democracy as a political regime. But even when recognized as the means, rather than an end of democracy, individual civil rights are seldom correctly traced to what makes sense of them as means.

Contemporary liberals and conservatives both profess support for the ideal of the greatest possible self-government as the most desirable feature of constitutional democracy, even as they contribute to this overlapping democratic consensus from opposite directions, as it were. The liberals celebrate democratic self-government by insisting on personal choices and praising multicultural pluralism. Less enthusiastic about either of these, the conservatives nevertheless promote the same ideal by calling for the minimal and decentralized state. From a nonpartisan perspective, these two approaches clearly complement each other. The ideal of maximum self-government, individual and social, is not easily imagined without a corresponding division of political authority into autonomous units.

To illustrate this liberal/conservative overlapping consensus on the desirability of social pluralism and political decentralization, we may juxtapose two historical-theoretical positions that Simon cites in separate contexts. The dates of these statements show that certain basic political insights have rather long lives, but that is not their most interesting aspect. What helps us acknowledge the desirability, and indeed the complementary nature of social pluralism and decentralized government, are the times and the identities of the writers recommending them. The defender of social pluralism speaking out about a century ago has impeccable conservative credentials, while the promoter of decentralized government is a certified liberal founder of the American experiment in democracy.

In the famous encyclical, *Rerum novarum*, Pope Leo XIII wrote as follows in 1896: "Let the state watch over these societies of citizens united together in the exercise of their rights, but let it not thrust itself into their peculiar concerns and their organization, for things move and live by the soul within them, and they may be killed by the grasp of a hand from without."[32] Clearly, today's liberals would not want to disagree, for what is here recommended is precisely diversity, choice, even multiculturalism. But it should be equally clear that this democratic social pluralism depends also on a corresponding organization of political government. And this is where the Pope's social pluralism is complemented by the political theory of no less a liberal democrat than Thomas Jefferson. "Were we directed from Washington when to sow, and when to reap," Jefferson writes, "we should soon want bread. It is by partition of cares, descending in gradation from general to particular, that the mass of human affairs may be best managed, for the good and prosperity of all."[33]

Now the historical and ideological switch these exemplary positions have apparently undergone could be seen as nothing more than another example of "how times have changed." What was once a liberal position is now a conservative principle, and vice versa. At a deeper level, however, this reversal points to a fundamental consensus that has over time shaped the theory and practice of modern constitutional democracy. Put in a nutshell, the ideal of self-government in democracy requires that all social tasks be performed by the smallest unit capable of handling them, and that the political authority at any level should step in only when absolutely necessary. In political theory, this is known as the principle of subsidiarity, and the democratic regime is supposed to be distinguished by its wholesale application, as it were. Democracy demands and makes possible the utmost self-government, political as well as individual and social. The autonomy of local government is part of the package that includes also personal rights, diversity, private property, free enterprise, freedom of association, etc. Now the contemporary liberals and conservatives may disagree on the order of priority among these items but not on their common foundation, which is none other than the principle of self-government. And the only thing this overlapping political consensus on the desirability of self-government lacks, is a fully adequate theory of government as such. For one cannot help suspecting that both sides still entertain the thought that if only "men were angels," no government would be necessary. That this simply is not so has been explained in the preceding chapter. It is liberty, that is, diversity and autonomy, that makes overall authority necessary, and it is this overall authority which in turn makes it all possible. What distinguishes democracy among political regimes is its use of the instruments of government.

INSTRUMENTS OF GOVERNMENT

Is democratic government ever entitled to use coercion? Some writers seem to believe that the use of coercion as an instrument of government is by definition undemocratic. Thus Rawls for one approaches this problem in the same way in which he approaches the question of civil disobedience: he simply assumes the government to be in the wrong. As recalled above, Rawls defends everyone's right to reject "socially approved rendering of the principles of justice" by implying that the next time around the "electorate as a whole" may well justify the action of those "civilly disobedient." In the meanwhile, Rawls argues, "there is no danger of anarchy as long as there is a sufficient working agreement in citizens' conception of justice and the conditions for resorting to civil disobedience are respected." But even as he concedes the possibility of divisive strife, Rawls cannot bring himself to grant that society may have the right to use coercion to protect itself. Instead, he blames the government. When "justified civil disobedience," not further specified, "seems to threaten civic concord," he writes,

> the responsibility falls not upon those who protest but upon those whose abuse of authority and power justifies such opposition. For to employ the coercive apparatus of the state in order to maintain manifestly unjust institutions is itself a form of illegitimate force that men in due course have a right to resist.[34]

As he avoids dealing with the citizens' moral obligation to obey *legitimate* government, Rawls has nothing to say about the state's use of coercion in maintaining *just* order. Having praised civil disobedience as a kind of superior moral category, Rawls logically must denounce state coercion as an "illegitimate force."

Self-government and coercion are clearly not complementary notions. But it is equally clear that ruling out coercion as an instrument of democratic government is utopian wishful thinking, if not worse. For there are also those who in the name of liberty condemn state coercion as nothing less than criminal violence. For instance, in his *The Constitution of Liberty*, Friedrich Hayek writes:

> *True* coercion occurs when armed bands of conquerors make the subject people toil for them, when organized gangsters extort a levy for 'protection' . . . and, *of course*, when the state threatens to inflict punishment and to employ physical force to make us obey its commands. [Italics supplied.][35]

Widely separated by their avowed political beliefs, Hayek and Rawls do not seem to be all that far apart on this issue. Ignoring the facts of human nature and the minimal requirements of life in common, they both denounce the use of coercion by democratic government as illegitimate. No less concerned with individual liberties, Simon has more respect for the lessons of experience.

The widely accepted textbook definition of the state as the social unit having the "monopoly" of ultimate force, or coercion, is, according to Simon, both superficial and misleading. The political association is correctly defined not by the means it may use but by its end which, as we have seen, is its natural rather than enforced monopoly: the pursuit of the common good. Toward this end, the state may use either of two instruments, persuasion or coercion. The democratic state prefers the former, but it is not forbidden from using the latter, as occasion may require. In fact, Simon thinks that all regimes have to depend at least as much on persuasion as on coercion. Communist or not, the Chinese government clearly cannot control its billion plus citizens by coercion alone. Yet to distinguish coercion from persuasion does present a challenge. In politics, as in interpersonal relations, psychic coercion can be as effective as physical coercion, and it is not always easy to tell it apart from genuine persuasion. Experience shows that both the crude massive propaganda of "the big lie" and the subtler advertising campaigns actually work to produce, without any visible threat of coercion, desired be-

liefs and preferences in the people they target. Methods considerably
short of "brainwashing" can still make voters choose a particular party
or candidate, while leaving them convinced that they have done it out
of their own free will. But even if they remain confused in practice,
the difference between psychic coercion and persuasion is no mystery.
Coercion is what causes action from the outside (by either physical or
psychic means); persuasion stimulates action from the inside of the person. The latter is the democratic instrument of choice. But that still does
not mean that democratic government may use coercion at most only to
restrain criminals from harming innocent people.[36]

Simon wonders about the people who hold coercion used by society morally dubious no matter what it is used for. After all, restraining a
criminal from engaging in criminal activities may well benefit the criminal no less than society. Calling prisons "correctional institutions" is not
entirely due to the modern addiction to euphemisms. Moreover, regardless of what one may think about its moral worth as an external aid in
reforming those who break the law, everyone should be able to recognize the value of coercion, or rather of the threat of coercion, at the
disposal of the political authority in helping ordinary, honest people to
remain honest. Why is it that the National Guard is regularly called out
to patrol areas hit by some natural disaster? They are sent to prevent
looting not by criminals but by yesterday's decent, churchgoing people
who may not be able to resist the temptation, when it appears that they
may get away with it, to appropriate something that does not belong to
them.[37] But why is it, then, that even while conceding that such threats
of force are necessary and useful, some are still reluctant to grant it any
moral worth? The answer is rather simple: Most people are reluctant to
admit to themselves that they obey the laws of the land not the least
because of the sanctions attached to them. But that is precisely the intent
behind legal sanctions: to minimize the need to apply them. Drafting a
practical Constitution, the American Framers had no illusions about it.
"Our own experience," Hamilton writes in *The Federalist* No. 28, "has
corroborated the lessons taught by the examples of other nations, that
the idea of governing at all times by the simple force of law (which we
are told is the only admissible principle of republican government) has
no place but in the reveries of those political doctors whose sagacity dis-
dains the admonitions of experimental instruction."[38] Thus, no matter
how civilized a society may be, or how democratic its government, it

can never dispense with coercion or the threat of coercion. In the real world, the rule of law will not work without it.

A related confusion permeating democratic political debates is the tendency to identify coercion with violence in opposition to justice. But, as Simon explains it, coercion and violence are not the same. They are distinct concepts and are clearly distinguishable in practice. Take, for instance, the so-called "frontier justice" practiced in the American West in the last century. The vigilantes who enforced this justice get mostly bad press today, but they must have at the least in some cases acted justly in protecting innocent lives and property. What they engaged in, however, was in all cases not coercion but violence. Their use of physical force may have been just, but they did not act "under the sanction of man-made law." The so-called "Wild West" bears a certain resemblance to Locke's "state of nature," where individuals have to fend for themselves in protecting what is theirs. In the state of civilization, however, legal coercion and threat of coercion replace "just violence" as an instrument of order. Coercion backing its laws, Simon writes, is "a legitimate instrument of an organized political community." When used as an instrument of positive law, physical coercion is not "violence." And to prevent all misunderstanding, Simon promptly specifies that "a so-called 'law,' " made to promote other than the common good, "is not genuinely a law." And that means that force in the service of such a law *is* violence.[39]

There is, however, one area of democratic life in common where, according to Simon, no kind of coercion must be allowed, and that is precisely its politics. Physically preventing some people from voting, which is known to happen sometime, is an obvious violation of this democratic principle. And so is also the absence of choice which used to guarantee the ruling communist parties those ridiculous percentages in their electoral victories. Yet not all potential violations of the democratic rule that prohibits any kind of coercion in its politics are so easily identified. For instance, electoral campaigns in the United States cost astronomical amounts of money. And as a consequence, not only some otherwise qualified candidates simply cannot afford to run for office; spending more millions of dollars than their opponents also taints the election of the winning candidates. These things are well known and are regularly criticized.[40] But Simon sees also the other side of this problem. Even though mass media advertising, positive or negative, may well involve potential psychic coercion, overregulating the electoral processes may also affect "from the outside" the peoples' freedom of choice. Thus rather than proposing a theoretical solution for problems pertaining to democratic elections, Simon believes that they are best left to what Hamilton calls "experimental instruction." Specific cases call for practical judgments.

In principle, then, the appropriate use of the instruments of government in democracy should be clear. Democracy prefers persuasion, but as a lawful political regime it is clearly entitled to use also coercion. It is only in its politics, in the process of establishing its government, that, as an elective regime, democracy must insist on the exclusive use of persuasion. Applying these two principles in practice is, of course, not a simple matter. But using them as guidelines, Simon suggests the following. For democratic government and society it is well worth to make extra efforts at persuasion even when legitimate coercion could settle the issue more promptly. For instance, police in democracy are supposed to be courteous and patient, and use coercion only as the last resort. Systemic preference for persuasion (hinting at a latent wish for unanimity) is also found in the multiple appeals and delays that characterize democratic judicial processes. Democratic justice cannot dispense with coercion, but it needs to use it carefully and sparingly. And when it comes to politics, democracy must rule out all coercion. Free and open elections can only be decided by persuasion. What these election and electoral debates should be about is, however, a separate issue.

CONSTITUTIONAL POLITICS

The requirement that attempts at persuading the voters must take place in free and open public discussions prompts Simon to raise once again the question of the link between democracy as a political regime and liberalism as a distinct ideology. Democracy, as we have seen, aspires to maximum political, social, and individual self-government. Liberalism may not be so easily defined to everyone's satisfaction, but Simon suggests as one of its defining characteristics, "the belief that the good of the social whole . . . is best procured by the spontaneous operation of elementary energies."[41] The familiar examples are the classical economic theory and its derivative, the free market of ideas. Now even though in modern times, democracy and liberalism have often enough been closely associated, Simon does not think that they are in themselves inseparable. After all, there was liberalism before democracy, and, as we shall see in the next chapter, one species of liberalism, namely, capitalism, could conceivably also survive democracy. In the present context, however, the question is what kind of issues can be sensibly expected to be settled by democratic elections. For Simon, the topics most suitable for political deliberations are ordinary laws and specific policies, that is, the available means toward agreed ends. Simon concedes, of course, that debates over political ends cannot always be completely avoided, because they cannot always be clearly separated from their means. In contrast to the typical liberal position that sees little harm in submitting everything to popular debate, Simon cautions against the risks this may involve.

In fact, considering desirable practice, even liberal writers hedge on the principle of wide open political debates with no-holds-barred. For instance, Rawls wants to insulate the search for a democratic "overlapping consensus" from all controversial philosophical topics. And Rorty, in his turn, is ready to exclude certain "vocabularies" and "interlocutors" from democratic political debates.[42] Simon takes a more precise stand. What he thinks is best for democracy is for its citizens not to raise fundamental constitutional questions every time they go to the polls. For example, that citizens must not be subject to arbitrary arrest is a principle, Simon holds, which pertains to the nature of any genuinely political association, while the indivisible nature of the Union of the American States is a fundamemtal principle of its Constitution. Democracy does not require that either of these principles be taken up in the free and open debates presupposed in democratic elections. As everyone knows, when the nature of the Union was taken up in political debate, the result was the Civil War. But let us also recognize that, if freedom from arbitrary arrest were to become an electoral issue in a democracy, we would have good reasons to be apprehensive about the fate of its liberal culture. In other words, liberalism as well as democracy may well be better off leaving alone not so much abstract philosophical topics as certain established political principles of their own making. It is granted that such abstinence may not be legally enforceable in democracy. Free speech in democracy extends in principle to its basic premises. But thoughtful democratic citizens could perhaps be persuaded not to bring fundamental constitutional principles up for debate "for light and transient reasons" or "for no reason at all except their sovereign pleasure."[43] Otherwise, an overlapping political consensus cannot be expected to work.

THE NEED TO GIVE

This chapter has surveyed in a rough way Simon's views on how the main theoretical principles of democracy are best applied in democratic practice toward the fulfillment of their intended purposes. Because popular sovereignty, the consent of the governed, universal suffrage, and majority rule do not in real life spontaneously support each other, they must be constantly adjusted to produce acceptable democratic results. To conclude this discussion, however, we need to look beyond its practical institutional arrangements to disclose the ultimate secret, as it were, of a successful constitutional democracy. For democracy is not only the form of political association best suited to satisfy the human need and potential for self-government. Democracy also provides all its citizens with an unmatched opportunity to practice what, if not the most common, is certainly a most excellent human virtue that both requires and complements our freedom. In democracy, everyone can satisfy his or her need to give. Such equal justice for all is not present in any other regime.

As Simon explains it, we all have "other centered" as well as "self-centered" needs. The simple notion of need "expresses merely the state of a tendency not yet satisfied with ultimate accomplishment." But the dynamism of the human psyche includes both self-centered and generous tendencies, and both of them admit of a state of need. These tendencies may change rank in different situations, but "the need to give is no less real than the need to take."[44] Self-centered needs have absolute priority in cases of destitution or privation. A thirsty person must have water, a sick person needs medical help, and a young person needs guidance. But what about the cases characterized by plenitude? What does a person need who is healthy, strong, intellectually accomplished, emotionally secure, and confident in his or her freedom? Inasmuch, Simon writes, as this "very state of accomplishment intensifies every generous trait and every tendency to act by way of superabundance," that person *needs* to give. The center of the act of giving remains, of course, always in the receiver of the gift, but that same act satisfies also a real need of the giver. We can easily imagine the frustrations of a talented artist, or a creative scientist, or indeed a natural-born leader deprived of opportunity to share with others what they have to offer. And these are only the most obvious examples. To understand how democracy excels in satisfying all human needs, we must recognize that every human being is secretly moved by the need to give. A homeless person sharing bread with a bird is a romantic but not necessarily an imaginary example of this human reality. In love and friendship, we need others to give of our love and friendship. And with regard to society as a whole, when this human tendency to act generously, which also means to act freely, is frustrated, it can easily become a formidable antisocial drive.[45] Not the least of the virtues of democracy, then, is that it works against strife and revolution precisely by allowing the widest scope not to the basest but to the noblest of human instincts and abilities. One can do nothing with either love or friendship, or wisdom for that matter, except give of it freely. Democracy both depends on it and, despite its necessary institutional qualifications, makes such acts of dedication accessible to all.

Because they have so little to say about generous human impulses, contemporary liberal writers distort both human nature and living democratic realities, let alone potential. In Montesquieu's tripartite division of regimes, monarchies operate on honor, despotisms on fear, and republics on "virtue."[46] Whatever else it may contain, this republican virtue must include the citizens' free mutual commitment to observe the rules they have established for themselves by means of republican institutions and procedures. Royal subjects comply with the king's wishes in expectation of "honors" he may bestow upon them. Under a tyrant, people subject themselves to his whims out of fear of punishment. But in a democracy, citizens are supposed to follow rules, to let their "conscience be bound" by their own free choice. Democratic citizens neither comply nor submit; they freely accept their civic duties. That such due acceptance does not violate their freedom may not be immediately clear to all, but Simon explains it well. Assuming that democratic government wills the common good, the citizens are not only set free to pursue their own particular goods. By supporting their elected government, they actively participate in the realization of that common good. Many theoretical as well as psychological confusions would be cleared up, Simon suggests, if the champions of individual freedoms would cease to express themselves "with systematic suspicion in respect to authority." Of course, like all things human, authority can be and is often abused. This is why auxiliary precautions are needed in practice in a democratic no less than in any other constitutional polity. But by and of itself the need for government is neither a necessary evil nor a lesser good. It is the only way to assure common action and the intention of the overall good of the community, both of which redound to the benefit and indeed the liberty of its members. To approach political authority with suspicion aforethought, then, risks "jeopardizing the sense of community and entering upon the road of individualistic revolt." But such a biased attitude results in an even worse harm, precisely because it hopelessly distorts our understanding of freedom. "A fixed attitude of opposition to authority," Simon writes, "is, essentially and not accidentally, the work of an arbitrary will. And *we have recognized in the arbitrary the supreme enemy of freedom*" (italics supplied).[47]

Taking up the cause of freedom normally involves the risk of minimizing the role of authority in political life. This tendency is the corollary of the common democratic dislike of hierarchy, which is seen as embodying the principle of authority in opposition to democratic equality. Yet the plain truth is that there is no hierarchy without autonomy, as there is no autonomy without authority. The principle of subsidiarity, by recommending social pluralism and decentralized government administration, recognizes explicitly these essential relations. But the idea and the ideal of a free democratic community is also nicely captured in the familiar motto of federalism, *e pluribus unum*. In fact, this notion of "diversity in unity" needs to be seen as the prototype of political association as such. The state, Aristotle holds against Plato, is by nature a plurality. Yet we are "many" only insofar as we are somehow united; otherwise we would only be singles, "ones," living lives "solitary, nasty, brutish, and short." Hobbes's mistake was that he identified such life with freedom, which logically led him to deny all freedom under the *Leviathan*. So it is well worth repeating that, being neither gods nor animals, human beings can fulfill their nature and achieve meaningful freedom only in communion with their fellow human beings. This is the common justification for all political regimes, as well as the ground for holding that democracy is the best of them all. True, no democratic constitution can guarantee that all its citizens will take advantage of their opportunities to achieve the kind of personal freedom required for responsible participation in democratic politics. All freedoms are apt to be abused perhaps even more than power and authority. And the ultimate freedom, as Simon reminds us, the freedom from the self, which rises above abuse, is also the hardest to achieve. What is not in doubt, however, is that constitutional democracy offers to all a chance to practice that kind of self-less freedom and to satisfy their need to give that is included with it. This may well be the profoundest reason why the people in democracy owe it above all to themselves to be responsible citizens.

NOTES

1. Yves R. Simon, *Philosophy of Democratic Government* (Chicago: University of Chicago Press, 1951), p. 73.

2. Ibid., p. 75n.

3. Alexandar Hamilton, John Jay, James Madison, *The Federalist* (New York: Modern Library, nd), No. 39, p. 243.

4. Ibid., p. 184.

5. Ibid., p. 145.

6. Ibid., p. 169. Simon reviews at some length also the interpretations of Belarmine and Cajetan, as well as that of Aquinas. The basic problem with sovereignty as power to bind consciences, as he sees it, is that, "on the one hand, it seems impossible to account for social life without assuming that man can bind the conscience of his neighbor; on the other hand, it is not easy to see how a man can ever enjoy such power." Ibid., p. 145.

7. *Theory of Justice*, pp. 389–91. See also comments by Elaine Spitz, *Majority Rule* (Chatham, NJ: Chatham House Publishers, 1984), p. 172.

8. See Stephen Holmes, *The Anatomy of Antiliberalism* (Cambridge, MA: Harvard University Press, 1993), ch. 10, "Indifference toward the Common Good?" and ch. 11, "The Eclipse of Authority?" In addition to Locke, Holmes quotes also Adam Smith, Hume, Kant, and Mill, to show that the traditional liberal political theorists insisted on political authority having both the right and adequate power to secure an orderly operation of society.

9. Sanford Levinson, *Constitutional Faith* (Princeton, NJ: Princeton University Press, 1988), p. 193.

10. *The Federalist* No. 49, p. 329.

11. See Stephen Holmes, *Passions and Constraint: On the Theory of Liberal Democracy* (Chicago: University of Chicago Press, 1995), p. 270.

12. *Democratic Government*, p. 194.

13. "[A]s each representative will be chosen by a greater number of citizens in the large than in the small republic, it will be more difficult for unworthy candidates to practice with success the vicious arts by which elections are too often carried; and the suffrages of the people being more free, will be more likely

to centre in men who possess the most attractive merit and the most diffusive and established characters." *The Federalist* No. 10, p. 60.

14. *Democratic Government*, p. 85.

15. Ibid., p. 89.

16. Ibid., p. 92.

17. Ibid., p. 97.

18. Yves R. Simon, *The Tradition of Natural Law* (New York: Fordham University Press, 1965, 1992), p. 164. The quotation is from S. E. Morrison and H. S. Commager, *The Growth of the American Republic* (New York: Oxford University Press, 1942), vol. 2, p. 175.

19. *Democratic Government*, pp. 99–101. For his critique of proportional representation, Simon draws heavily on Ferdinand A. Hermens, *Democracy or Anarchy?* (Notre Dame, IN: University of Notre Dame Press, 1941).

20. *Democratic Government*, pp. 102. Simon quotes from *The Federalist* No. 22, where Hamilton writes: "The necessity of unanimity in public bodies, or something approaching toward it, has been founded upon a supposition that it would contribute to security. But its real operation is to embarrass the administration, destroy the energy of government, and to substitute the pleasure, caprice, or artifices of an insignificant, turbulent, or corrupt junto to the regular deliberations and decisions of a respectable majority."

21. *Democratic Government*, pp. 107.

22. *The Federalist* No. 9, p. 47.

23. A faction, according to Madison, is any group "adverse to the rights of other citizens, or to the permanent and aggregate interests of the community." If the group constitutes a minority, majority rule will take care of it. But if a majority turns into a faction "pure (direct) democracy" is helpless to check it. A republic is better off, because its scheme of representation tends to "refine and enlarge public views." And a large republic, with many competing interests, is almost sure to "prevent the impulse and the opportunity" to form majority faction from coinciding. *The Federalist* No. 10.

24. *The Federalist* Nos. 10 and 51.

25. See James MacGregor Burns, *The Deadlock of Democracy* (Englewood Cliffs, NJ: Prentice-Hall, 1963).

26. *Democratic Government*, p. 132.

27. Ibid., pp. 136–37.

28. Yves R. Simon, *The Community of the Free* (New York: Henry Holt, 1947), p. 166.

29. *The Federalist* No. 10, p. 55.

30. *Democratic Government*, p. 139.

31. "Congress shall make no laws. . . ." In contrast to the language of the American Bill of Rights, most twentieth-century constitutions promise freedom of assembly, together with rights to employment, health care, etc.

32. Quoted by Simon in *Democratic Government*, p. 130.

33. Quoted by Simon in *General Theory of Authority* (Notre Dame, IN: University of Notre Dame Press, 1962, 1980), p. 138.

34. Rawls, *A Theory of Justice*, pp. 389–91.

35. Friedrich Hayek, *The Constitution of Liberty* (Chicago: University of Chicago Press, 1960), p. 37.

36. *Democratic Government*, pp. 115–19.

37. Ibid., pp. 108ff; *Natural Law*, pp. 35–36.

38. Quoted in *Democratic Government*, p. 115n.

39. *Democratic Government*, pp. 112–13.

40. See Frank J. Sorauf, *Inside Campaign Finance: Myths and Realities* (New Haven, CT: Yale University Press, 1992). Also Herbert E. Alexander, *Financing Politics: Money, Elections, and Political Reform* (Washington, DC: Congressional Quarterly Press, 1992).

41. *Democratic Government*, p. 122.

42. See above pp. 80–82.

43. In 1777, an American pamphleteer boasted as follows: "I define civil liberty to be not a 'government by laws,' made agreeable to charters, bills of rights or compacts, but a power existing in the people at large, at any time, for any cause, or for no cause, but their own sovereign pleasure, to alter or annihilate both the mode and essence of any former government, and adopt a new one in its stead." Quoted in Edward S. Corwin, *The Higher Law Background of American Constitutional Law* (Ithaca, NY: Cornell University Press, 1959), p. 88.

44. *General Theory of Authority*, p. 24.

45. *Democratic Government*, p. 308.

46. Montesquieu, *The Spirit of Laws*, Book III, "Of the Principles of the Three Kinds of Government."

47. *Community of the Free*, p. 31.

5

THE COMMUNITY OF THE FREE

Democracy needs a sensible constitution and citizens loyal to it, but that is not all it needs. Its specific claim to being first among political regimes, based on maximum self-government, includes the promise that the liberty and equality guaranteed by its constitution will not be limited exclusively to politics. Under a democratic constitution, one would rightly expect, also, a democratic society and even something like a democratic culture. In fact, that is precisely what Tocqueville saw in America and predicted would spread from the United States to all parts of the world. And he was right. The practices may vary, but the trend is unmistakable. Women now vote in Switzerland as well as in Pakistan, and Afro-Americans are elected to office in the State of Mississippi. Of course, gender and racial discrimination is far from having been completely eliminated everywhere, but its theory finds few public defenders. Officially, as it were, democratic liberty and equality are "in." And yet, the spirit of the times appears somewhat less then enthusiastic about further democratic progress. Why? As suggested in chapter 2, the strange fashions in postmodern philosophy certainly have something to do with it. The deconstruction of its rational foundations is clearly not designed to boost confidence in democratic government from common reflection and choice. Doubts about the future of democracy, however, are generated also and more directly by two other closely related developments: the ever more sophisticated technology and the global spread of capitalism.

For instance, while the transfer of technology has enabled some of the so-called Third World countries to become major players in the world economy, they have not become visibly more democratic. Those countries are capitalist but not democratic. Moreover, the experiments with capitalism and democracy in the former communist countries in Europe are not going too well. And despite general prosperity in the United States, the leading democratic country with the most advanced technology and capitalist economy, the gap between the rich and the poor is widening with each subsequent survey. In short, the ideal of liberty, equality, and justice for all is not exactly keeping up with capitalist free enterprise and technological progress.[1]

The historical connection between democracy, modern economic practices, and modern technology may be traced symbolically to the year 1776, which saw the publication of both the Declaration of Independence and *The Wealth of Nations* and witnessed radical improvements in the steam engine. What happened afterwards is open to interpretation, but no one can deny that there was much conflict and confusion. The record shows capitalism and technology racing ahead of democracy and causing great social dislocations, misery, and protest. Now the present conditions in the advanced liberal democratic countries may appear to lend some credence to the view that all those conflicts and sufferings were the unfortunate but perhaps unavoidable costs leading to the eventual joint triumph of free enterprise market economy, advanced technology, and democratic politics. A less ideological perspective, however, suggests a rather different scenario, not only for its history but also for what democracy may face in the future. The coexistence of democracy with capitalism and technology in the leading Western countries, far from being predestined or due to some essential affinity between them, is in fact the result of continuous adjustments in political and economic theories and practices. History does not show democracy, capitalism, and modern technology spontaneously reinforcing each other. Nor does the future promise that democracy can continue to grow and develop, or even keep its gains, without struggle.

In the same year in which Marx and Engels published their manifesto proclaiming the beginning of the end of capitalism, in the Preface to the twelfth edition of his own classic speculation about the political future of the world, Tocqueville found it relevant to ask: "Can it be believed that the democracy which has overthrown the feudal system and vanquished kings will retreat before tradesmen and capitalists?"[2] Since then, democracy has emerged victorious against both fascism and communism and has indeed not retreated before the capitalists either. But to attribute that felicitous outcome to some inherent attraction between democracy and capitalism, or technology, both betrays history and endangers democratic future. For there was conflict, there is conflict, and we cannot assume that the conflict between the demands of capitalist economics and the aspirations of democratic politics, mostly over the control of technology, will end soon.

In his imposing *The Spirit of Democratic Capitalism*, Michael Novak some years ago marshaled facts, figures, and subtle arguments from several fields, including theology, to support his thesis that democracy and capitalism together are the key to "the spiritual wealth of nations."[3] This seems indeed to be the prevailing, almost an "official" position in the United States, loudly proclaimed especially in foreign policy statements (though not necessarily followed in practice). But as one would expect in a democracy, contrary opinions also abound. For instance, in the new edition of their popular book entitled, *Habits of the Heart*, what the editors call "the hegemony of the neoconservative ideology" is blamed, together with the capitalist economy, for all sorts of social ills, including sharpening of class distinctions and the spreading of "cancerous" individualism.[4] Similar complaints are voiced in another recent book entitled *Democracy and Capitalism*. Noting the failure of socialism as well as the shortcomings of capitalism, its authors want to explore a "visionary historical alternative," which they call "postliberal democracy."[5] They argue as follows. Whereas some may consider the talk about democracy and capitalism being at the crossroads unduly alarmist, there are sound reasons not to dismiss lightly the concerns that have inspired such talk.[6] Besides being a system of exchange, capitalism is also a system of employment, and a democratic society clearly cannot be indifferent to a situation in which most citizens depend on a smaller number of other citizens to give them jobs to make a living.[7] (In *Habits of the Heart*, these job-dependent citizens are called the "anxious class.") But democracy in company with capitalism has an even deeper problem. The liberal political ideology on which contemporary democracy relies for theoretical support operates strangely apart from the liberal economic theory which supports capitalism. Dealing with power, the former ignores economics, while the latter does not have much to say about politics.[8] Using Marxist errors for comparison, the authors explain the situation as follows:

> Progressive social change in the liberal democratic societies has followed the logic of collective opposition to oppression suggested by

Marxian theory, while adopting the liberal language of rights and of the democratic empowerment . . . [Thus] liberalism gives us the discourse of social change, whereas Marxism gives us the theory of social change. Social change itself, however, is opaque to both liberalism, which does not recognize that its discourse developed through class and other collective struggles, and to Marxism, which misconstrues what these struggles were for.[9]

The major fault of liberalism, then, "lies not in overstating the possibilities of human freedom, but in failing to identify the roots of domination—those which lie in economic dependency . . . [while at the same time] elevating a radically individual conception of autonomy to the detriment of a conception of community which might be the basis of democratic empowerment."[10]

We have seen in a previous chapter how Simon handles the second, call it the political, part of this not uncommon critique of liberalism. Humans are by nature social and political beings, and there can be no society without government. Moreover, according to Simon, various forms of government democracy provide for the most rewarding exercise of both political authority and political liberty. Because democratic liberty is inseparable from democratic equality, any kind of social or economic dependence necessarily represents a threat to both. This is why Simon takes the right of private property to be not just equal to the freedom of religion, of assembly, and of expression but to be, in real life, their practical foundation. Recognizing the right to private property upholds at the same time both the social and the political liberty and equality. But that does not mean that great disparities in wealth make no difference in democracy, and Simon finds minimizing their potential harm a rather disturbing feature of the "democratic complacency in our time." Combined with the capitalist system of employment, the gap between the rich and the poor in modern capitalist society recalls the institutionalized human bondage that modern democracy had to overcome at its birth.[11]

WHAT REALLY HAPPENED IN HISTORY

Simon believes that the development of modern democracy is best understood as divided in two stages, which we may here call legal and social.[12] Put simply, the focus in the first stage was on liberty, while in the second stage the focus has shifted to equality. What both the American and the French Revolutions proclaimed was that the political government must be the government of the free, the opposite of any kind of master-servant relationship. Thus the history of democracy begins with the abolition of feudalism and serfdom, and to the extent that no country today recognizes legal servitude, this first stage in the development of modern democracy may be considered closed.

The beginning dates of its second stage vary greatly from country to country, as does its progress. In the United States, the movement toward more social (if not also economic) equality is associated with the Presidency of Andrew Jackson and (leaving aside Lincoln and the Civil War) with the much later Presidencies of the two Roosevelts. In Great Britain, the Reform Act of 1832 may have doubled the electorate, but it was not until about a century later, after the Second World War, that the well-established customary distinction between the classes began to crumble. The democratization of the German society proceeded likewise at its own pace. And so on, in Italy, Spain, Sweden, etc. The political content, however, of this second stage in the progress of modern democracy is not in doubt, and Simon finds it, together with its date, marked most clearly in France. What took place in Paris between February and July of 1848, he suggests, symbolizes the historic transition from the politics of liberty to the politics of equality.[13] The defeat of Napoleon in 1815 was followed by the Restoration under two Bourbon kings, and then, from 1830, by the rule of "the Citizen-King," Louis Philip of Orleans. But in February 1848, there was a small revolution in Paris, and the Second Republic was proclaimed by an alliance of representatives from the middle and the working classes acting in unison. Six months later, however, this alliance broke up and the former political allies had a violent confrontation. The French workers lost that battle but not, as the saying goes, the war. Allowing for the widest national variations and degrees of intensity (including American exceptionalism), the competition for political power between parties defending, on the one hand, the interests of the propertied classes and, on the other hand, the interests of the ever growing number of people who have to work for others to make a living has in fact remained the focus of modern history and politics ever since.

After the First and the Second World Wars, the communists came to power in a number of countries and proclaimed the victory of the working classes. But like the alleged class reconciliation decreed between the two wars by the Nazis and the Fascists at the expense of democracy, what the workers actually experienced in the Soviet Union and the other communist countries was more like a betrayal. The workers did receive social recognition and their standard of living did improve, but they paid for it with personal freedoms. By contrast, over the same period, the workers in the established democratic countries with capitalist economies were able, mostly by democratic means, both to raise their standard of living and to expand their civil liberties. To keep the history of modern democracy straight, however, and in order not to compromise its chances for further improvement, the causes of this happy outcome must be identified correctly. The political victories of the common people are the fruits of their prolonged struggles not only against the practices of Tocqueville's "tradesmen and capitalists" but also against the domination of the classical economic theory. The reason why the people in democratic societies today can boast of greater liberty, equality, and justice for all is that they have succeeded in forcing both capitalist practice and capitalist theory to adjust to their demands. This change did not come about as if guided by an "invisible hand." It is the result of a protracted challenge against both the practice and the theory of capitalism.[14] And what is more, this struggle was inspired largely by socialist thinkers and movements. As Simon sees it,

> several trends and aspirations which play a major part in the dynamism of our societies have achieved self-consciousness in socialist doctrines. Consequently, whether the solutions proposed by socialism should be received or rejected, the problems it has raised cannot be ignored. It is clearly indicated that democracy should reconsider the problems raised by socialism, and work out solutions of its own.[15]

Among these problems, Simon points to the rise of huge private commercial, industrial, and financial corporations, which has placed in private hands a power quite capable of challenging the authority of the democratic state.[16] The socialist solution, requiring state control of economics, may have worked in part in some places, but Simon does not recommend it. Combining political and economic powers in the same hands multiplies enormously the temptation to abuse. Thus in Simon's opinion, the influence of corporate capitalism in democracy is best checked by the countervailing power of various citizens' organizations, including especially labor unions and cooperative enterprises of producers and consumers.[17]

The cause of democracy was also helped by socialist thinkers when they exposed and refuted the traditional conservative charge that the democracy of the common people promoted hedonistic materialism at the expense of spiritual values. Lusting after material goods, eagerly provided by capitalist enterprise, does seem to have kept pace with the development of democracy. But this modern mass "materialism" has also a more respectable explanation, which was first formulated by socialist thinkers. Scarcity of the necessities of life had been, with rare exceptions, the normal human condition for most of history, and people had become more or less resigned to it. But that historical condition, which could not be helped by any system of distribution, has in fact been overcome through modern technology. Today, it is possible to produce material goods in abundance, and often enough they are so available. Consequently, if some people still suffer deprivation, this can no longer be blamed on the nature of things. The condition is traceable primarily to faulty distribution. Thus "the enjoyment of wealth by the happy few," Simon writes, has assumed "a new significance in our times." It has become "evidence of a mismanagement which perpetuates destitution at a time when physical environment of human existence has ceased to make it unavoidable."[18] Responding to democratic protests, capitalism has in fact changed its ways, but its past must not be simply forgotten. Pouring milk into gutters (while many children went without it), or burning coffee as fuel, in order to keep their prices up, as happened during the Great Depression, proves to Simon that widespread destitution in the midst of plenty cannot be excluded as an unintended consequence of the capitalist free-market economy. Nor will it do to blame these things on technology alone.[19] In Simon's opinion, if they are to serve human, humane, and democratic purposes, neither technology nor capitalism can be left totally unchecked.

Simon saves for last what he considers to be the most relevant socialist contribution to the modern search for a just democratic society. By insisting that justice matters in economics no less than in politics, the socialist thinkers, according to Simon, have decisively enlightened the moral conscience of our time. While opinions differ widely as to what can be done about it, today most people recognize that gross economic inequalities and relations of dependency bear directly on the quality of democratic politics and prospects. As noted above, Simon explicitly rejects the socialist planning and leveling solutions. Private enterprise and private property are good for democracy as is also diversity in income and holdings. Thus capitalism and democracy are by no means incompatible. But that does not mean that further development of democratic politics would not be helped by more democratic economics. What is interesting is that the suggestion Simon offers on how to promote democratic economics is derived from a two-thousand-year-old theory.

BASIC ECONOMIC JUSTICE

Today most people would agree that the principle of "one man, one vote" expresses an essential requirement of democratic politics. But there is no comparable agreement on what would be the true mark of democratic albeit capitalist economics. The old-time liberals and today's neoconservatives continue to recommend free enterprise and free market, while the contemporary liberals and various socialists, heeding the lessons of history, invoke the need for democratic control of at least the most important economic transactions. In reality, all democratic nations have by now introduced such things as an official basic interest rate, minimum wage legislation, collective bargaining by labor unions, unemployment compensation, subsidies to agriculture, some control of insurance premiums, plus all sorts of licensing and authorization of professions and businesses, and so on. And despite the current popularity of deregulation and privatization, no one really expects a return to the freewheeling practices of the Gilded Age of capitalism. Consequently, rather than over the grand principles, politicians argue about details, e.g., by how many cents to increase the minimum wage over what period of time. Simon approaches the problems of "democratic economics" at another level.

The economic counterpart of the principle "one man one vote," which is supposed to assure liberty, equality, and democratic political justice for all, is, according to Simon, an equally simple rule, namely, *equality in exchange*. Trying to promote economic justice by means of planned economies and by leveling possessions and incomes is not the least among socialist errors. As has by now been confirmed by history, such policies produce new privileged bureaucracies and frustrate individual initiatives, which together not only contradict democratic aspirations but also hinder economic development. Democracy is supposed to promote, rather than eliminate, autonomy and diversity in the economic as well as in other pursuits. Indeed, without recognizing the all too human inclination to acquire worldly goods, the promise of happiness its famous equality formula adds to life, liberty, and the consent of the governed would be but an empty slogan. The material goods may be in the third place on the classical list, after the goods of the mind and the goods of the body—wisdom and health—but that does not mean that material goods do not satisfy real and legitimate human needs and desires. To assume, then, that economic planning and equalization of possessions will make for economic justice is both utopian and undemocratic. But there is one equality requirement that is as decisive for democratic economics as the principle of "one man, one vote" is for democratic politics. Calling this requirement "equality in exchange," Simon makes modern economic and political sense by relying on Aristotle's notion of "commutative justice."[20]

Ideally, what the competition in the free market is supposed to assure is precisely that the goods are traded for what they are worth. This aspect of the classical economic theory conforms to the rule of commutative justice, which stipulates that the only just exchange between two parties is an equal exchange. When you get what you pay for, the seller also gets what his goods are worth. Of course, calculating such equivalences involves indefinitely many practical difficulties, and Simon readily concedes that, all other things being equal, the time-honored solution of leaving the actual prices up to the buyers and sellers in the market is not altogether unreasonable.[21] Still, since in real life no market operates under perfect competition, the rule of equal exchange is in effect set aside by the law of supply and demand, which often produces harmful, even if not intended, social consequences. For instance, an abundant catch may ruin independent small fishermen by causing the price of fish to fall below what it costs to catch them and bring them to market. Or, when jobs are scarce, workers may have to accept a wage that is less than what their work is worth, or even less than what they need merely to subsist.[22] Now there was a time, and not so long ago, when such happenings were dismissed with a shrug of "tough luck" not only by the capitalists who profited from them but also by the academic exponents of "social Darwinism." That this is no longer the case shows how much modern social conscience has improved. Today, all democratic governments are prepared to intervene when their market economies threaten to get out of control, and Simon considers this development a victory not for socialism but for the democracy of the common people. These corrective measures may do no more than approximate the ideal of equal justice in economic transactions, but they clearly show that laissez-faire economics does not work for the good of all as claimed by its theory.

Simon has no specific policies to recommend, but the principle of equal exchange as the economic counterpart of political justice of "one man, one vote" provides a valuable guideline for promoting democratic economics. For as Simon explains it, there is something truly wonderful about justice in exchange: An equal exchange affirms and upholds at the same time both the *equality* and the *freedom* of the parties involved. Subject to the contingencies of real-life experiences, liberty and equality do not always support each other. But in every equal exchange they become, in joint denial of exploitation and without fail, one and the same.[23] Exploitation, whether it shows up in politics or in economics, does not negate liberty and equality separately or selectively. Exploitation destroys their oneness and breeds alienation. To keep liberty and equality together, therefore, democracy must be concerned no less with economic than with political justice. The free-market economy may be practical and convenient, and it is by no means always inequitable. In fact, alternative systems have proven worse. But there is one thing that for its own protection democracy cannot permit. If it is to remain the community of the free, democracy must not let the law of supply and demand become the supreme law of the land.

SOCIAL JUSTICE

Again, contingent as its application may be, the classical economic theory is not absurd. Assuming free competition among many buyers and sellers, the price of goods on the market could be expected to approximate their cost, and their sale would then tend to satisfy the rule of equality in exchange and thus affirm also the freedom of the parties involved. But quite apart from the nonexistence of such an ideal free market, the classical economic theory itself is grossly prejudicial in explaining how that market is supposed to work. In calculating the fair value of the commodities exchanged in the market, this theory does not treat all "goods" equally, and the exception it claims gives its bias away. Thus, even as it holds human labor to be just another commodity to be sold and bought on the market, the classical economic theory (and the practice it has inspired) in effect denies the sellers of labor what it grants all other sellers. The fair value of the goods on the theoretical free market is assumed to include a margin of "profit" for all except the laborers. The producers' and the sellers' prices are calculated to include a certain amount over and above their actual cost. Competition may keep that amount to a minimum, but this cannot be zero, since the whole system, not including the sellers of labor, operates, after all, on "the profit motive". Producers will not produce, and sellers will not sell, if there is no profit in it. But under the classical theory's "iron law of wages," the most the sellers of labor are entitled to is what enables them "one with another, to subsist and perpetuate their race, without either increase or diminution."[24] In other words, in contrast to all other prices, the ideal price of labor on the classical free market is not calculated to include any margin of "profit." And the practical reason for it, duly acknowledged in classical economic theory, is simply that the sellers of labor have a more pressing motive to compete in the free market, namely, naked survival. Now it is true that this alleged "natural law" of economics is seldom openly invoked today. Some economists, and politicians, may still argue that legislating a minimum wage is "uneconomical," but even the staunchest defenders of capitalism desist from denouncing it as "unnatural," let alone "immoral." This is another sign of democratic progress. But that progress has by no means eliminated all the blind spots so common to social consciences.

If economic justice demands strict equality in exchange, and especially that no one should be paid less than what one's work is worth, or what one needs to live, does it not follow necessarily that no one should be paid more than what one's work or service is worth, or indefinitely more than one needs to live well? Simon has no doubts about it. He writes:

> Just as we have come to outlaw destitution, which was still considered an inescapable phase of the economic cycle three generations ago, so

a day will come when the conscience of the just will recognize that the recompense of human labor, though admitting of inequalities, is comprised between a lower limit, which cannot be very low . . . and an upper limit, which cannot be very high—for no aspect of the common good demands that any person should enjoy an income many times greater than his avowable need.[25]

This may well be the touchiest point for the defenders of strict capitalist economics, even after two more generations have passed since Simon wrote the above lines. While they may grudgingly concede the political usefulness of a legislated minimum wage, they draw the line at tinkering with the maximum. And because this is such a touchy point, it is important to establish that economic leveling is not what Simon has in mind. For instance, if a family of four can have a decent life on an income of $4,000 (in 1947 dollars), and another family has an income of $100,000, Simon asks, how should we calculate the real difference between their situations. Because the first family has "enough" for a decent life, the $96,000 more the second family has to spend is for Simon only of secondary importance. And so, rather than as 25:1, he finds the real difference between their two situations to be more like 125:100.[26]

As in many other contexts, however, the difference in quantity does here, too, translate into difference in quality—and raises questions about the direction in which contemporary capitalist economy may be moving. Thus when we learn that the gap between the compensations of some top corporate executives in the United States and the compensation of their lowest paid workers has now widened to 225:1, it is not only our ordinary moral sensitivity that should be offended. In dollars, this means that some CEOs collect $4,500,000, while the majority of their employees get about $20,000—a difference of $4,480,000! In comparing these incomes, Simon's suggested mathematical formula is worse than useless, for no degree of charity could justify representing the actual gap between those two incomes as 325:100.[27] Thus even if there were no longer any citizens struggling to make the ends barely meet, just having some—including entertainers and sports figures—amass wealth approximating that of the old feudal lords, or of the "robber barons" of the Gilded Age, does not augur well for the future of democracy.[28] Even if the capitalist tide were to raise all boats (which it does not), there is no reason for democrats to cheer, if that tide also makes some yachts airborne, as it were. Nor will it do to argue that under "democratic capitalism" anyone has a fair chance to "make it." Billionaires are no asset to democracy, and as more of them are produced, the more reasons there are to worry about the future.[29]

A related issue of social justice on which democratic opinion and conscience remain confused is "the welfare state." Simon firmly believes that all people able to do so should earn their keep by honest work (for which they should be justly compensated). But what, he asks, about old people, sick people, mentally ill people; what about victims of accidents at work and elsewhere; what about widows; what about crippled children; what about orphans? In the simpler societies of times past, if the parents died while their children were still young, it may not have been unusual for some neighbors to take care of the orphans. In today's mobile, mass, urban society, however, such neighborly initiative is not likely, which makes it imperative that the help to the needy be organized and provided institutionally. Given choice, Simon would prefer this help to be provided by nongovernmental organizations, which could be assumed to operate more efficiently than any state bureaucracy. But Simon has no doubts about the moral responsibility of modern society, with ample means at its disposal, to provide assistance to its members who might need it. This requirement may be said to come under the distributive part of political justice. A decent society *owes* each and every one of its members his or her due according to either merit or need. Thus the counterpart of the honors to the deserving is the help to the needy. Equal exchange among individuals may take care of economic justice among equals, but it will not satisfy all the requirements of comprehensive social justice, which covers also the unequal, so to speak. In this life of contingencies, there will always be people who have little or nothing to offer in exchange, and in their case political justice requires distribution according to need. Simon sees the gradual recognition of this responsibility as part of the historical progress in the cognition of Natural Law. Involved here is more than just our feelings of sympathy for those less fortunate. Compassion may give us a push, so to speak, but at issue here is the objective understanding of the human condition that transcends specific historical situations. To put it bluntly, there is nothing wrong with the notion of "the welfare state." The political association is, after all, a kind of mutual benefit society, and perhaps especially so when organized democratically. But help for fellow citizens in need, according to Simon, is not just what would be nice for a democratic society to provide. To do so, Simon writes, is right "by reason of human nature and by reason of the contingency to which human nature is exposed."[30] Under modern conditions of life, this help must be provided by public institutions.

THEORY VERSUS PRACTICE

Finally, something needs to be said also about the obvious discrepancy between the value-neutral pretensions of the prevailing economic "science" and the living practice of the so-called free-market societies. Economists would rather forget about it, but the true relation between economics and politics is daily confirmed by generally recognized exceptions to free enterprise and its law of supply and demand. Why is it that some products of which there is supply and for which there is demand are banned in most countries of the world and their trade suppressed by international agreements? Cocaine is the prime example, but the list of forbidden goods is by no means limited to drugs or even just to things that may be harmful to human beings. Banning ivory from international trade is intended to save the elephants, other exclusions to save the whales, rhinoceroses, eagles, etc. And what about fluorcarbon aerosol propellants banned in order to save the ozone layer, climate, environment, the world? These measures taken in response to the recognition of the physical unity of the world harken back to the original meaning of "economics," namely, the managing of scarce resources for the benefit of the family unit. More directly, the prohibition of trade in drugs confirms that not all "goods" are equal, and that before being admitted to the "free" market, things are in fact evaluated with respect to their utility, use, and service to human beings.

Perhaps no example illustrates better the hypocrisy, or at least the inconsistency, of the upholders of the free enterprise and free-market dogmas than the recent legal settlements with the tobacco companies. Even though their product is bought freely and legally on the open market, the American tobacco companies have been eager to negotiate compensation for the harm tobacco is said to cause to people who choose to use it. Now the main reason the tobacco executives are willing to settle may well be "economic": They would like to pay as little as possible. But the whole affair illustrates dramatically what everybody has always known: Just because it is freely and legally sold and bought in the market does not qualify a product as a *human good.*

The truth of the matter is that quite apart from things physically harmful to human beings, or other species, or the environment, the market supplies illusory services and unneeded goods in abundance. Simon wonders about cars with more power than will ever be used, about piles upon piles of neckties in department stores, expensive cosmetics with debatable aesthetic or health benefits, and so on, to which we may add the more recent dubious offers of psychological and spiritual help which have acquired a permanent niche on national television. And since all such products and services are being pushed by massive advertising, additional natural as well as human resources are continually wasted. Moreover, the profit-driven economy often tends to "expand" at the expense of affordable housing, or efficient public transportation, not to mention decent health care for everyone. To say it again, then, not only the claim that free enterprise market economy guarantees liberty, equality, and justice for all but also the claim that the market is "free" are equally false. As Simon sees it, totally unchecked capitalism cannot avoid errors concerning the cost of production, which lead to inequality in exchange, rupture of balance, and alienation.[31] And this is why democracy cannot dispense with value judgments in its economics any more than in its politics. Simon puts it as follows: No economic theory can do without a concept of wealth; no concept of wealth is intelligible without some reference to use or service; and all reference to use or service leads to questions of what is good for man. His job as a philosopher, Simon writes, bids him to raise doubts about the obviousness of the economists' value-neutral, supply-demand empiricism.[32] Without clarifying questions of economic justice, it is futile to try to calculate democracy's overall prospects.

The tension between the claims of liberal capitalist ideology and the democratic political aspirations, however, is not the only problem that stands in the way of progress toward better understanding of the human good that favors democracy. The hopes of strengthening individual freedom and social self-government depend today also on coming to terms with the power of modern technology. Marx was wrong about capitalism being doomed because, forced by competition to innovate forever its machines, its main product would be the impoverished proletarians bent on establishing a new radically egalitarian democratic society.

Today, due mainly to its applying the latest scientific-technological inventions in its production, capitalism is thriving around the globe, and it is not exactly spreading misery. But even assuming capitalist economic practices brought under control, that does not mean that technology would cease to be a problem for democracy.

DEMOCRACY AND TECHNOLOGY

The long list of critics discussing the meaning and the role of technology in modern experience includes such well-known names as Jacques Ellul, Martin Heidegger, Hannah Arendt, C. S. Lewis, Erich Fromm, Theodor Adorno, Max Horkheimer, Hans Jonas, among others. These writers do not all judge its impact in exactly the same way, but they all tend to treat technology as in some sense an autonomous force posed to "take over," if it had not already done so.[33] From being a way of thinking (how to get things done), some writers have come to believe that technology has become for modern mankind, for better or worse, a way of being. Most are not happy about it, but no one claims to know exactly how that condition could be changed.

For instance, Heidegger holds what he calls "technicity," as distinguished from techniques, to be at the same time "the epochal stamp" and the "unconcealing" of the age. What that means is best left, together with his speculations about "the singularity and the tragedy of Being," to the experts. But his often quoted line that "technology is the danger that saves" could perhaps be taken to mean that, uniquely problematic as it is, the modern situation of man is not hopeless.[34] Whether this is good or bad for democracy, Heidegger does not say. But according to one interpreter at least, Heidegger does give liberty a chance—of sorts. As a frame of thinking, this commentator argues, technology undoes metaphysical rationalism, and as a specific self-conscious and multidimensional information form it also replaces the linear, blind, hierarchical order imposed by old mechanical devices. Thus in both instances technology "saves" by promoting the possibility of "weak ontology" and expanding thereby the range of personal and political liberty.[35]

Now tracing liberty to a "weak ontology" recalls both Lucretius' notion of the unaccountable atomic "swerve" and Eddington's half-joke about the uncertainty principle enlightening physicists about the meaning of freedom.[36] Apparently, Heidegger, too, identifies freedom with indetermination. Technology has given modern mankind the power to do what had never been done before, and there is no reason to think that there is a specified end to further expansion of that power. Eventually, then, technology might let us do virtually *anything* we want. But is not that precisely the danger rather than the salvation of technology? If it can be done, it will be done, regardless! Simon traces the problems with technology to the modern obsession with "the conquest of nature," originally recommended by both Francis Bacon and René Descartes, fanned by the Industrial Revolution, and solemnized, as it were, in our time by prospects of space travel as well as by the unraveling of the human genetic code. And it remains to be seen how this "conquest of nature" may be reconciled with the democratic pursuit of liberty, equality, and self-government.[37]

Simon opens his discussion of the relations between democracy and technology by drawing our attention to a well-known double paradox. Even though the United States has become the most technologized and urbanized country in the world, its citizens still seem to cherish the ideal of rural democracy, in a community of independent small farmers, an ideal proposed by Thomas Jefferson, a large land and slave owner. And what Simon finds behind this conflict of ideals and reality is a deeply rooted suspicion that a technological society does not favor democratic government.[38] Technological society, on this view, is suspected of encouraging the lust for power, inviting mores of servitude, and spreading individualistic loneliness, in contrast to the pursuit of happiness, individual self-government, and community feelings, expected to prevail in a democratic community of independent farmers. Simon finds much truth in these contrasts, and he believes that the symbols of rural democracy and the family farm represent valuable moral and psychological counterweights to the pressures of life dominated by technology. But he has no illusions about the decisive impact of technology on modern experience.

Simon defines technology as "a rational discipline designed to assure the mastery of man over physical nature through the application of scientifically determined laws." As such, technology is indifferent to the use made of it. One may have the technology and not use it; and one may use it either rightly or wrongly, not only from an ethical point of view but also from the point of view of the technique itself. A grammarian, as Aristotle notes, is best qualified to make grammatical mistakes. A chemist, Simon adds, is best qualified to sabotage a chemical plant.[39] But this is technique considered in the abstract. In its human and social existence, technology does acquire definite tendencies relative to its use. Ancient Greeks, and the Chinese, are reputed to have refrained, for whatever reason, from turning their scientific knowledge into technology for everyday use. But that choice is no longer available to modern mankind, who has come to depend on the continuous development of technology not just for the good life but for life itself. And so, Simon readily acknowledges that "the first law of a technological society is a tendency to remain technological." Such a society may be in many respects frightening, but Simon insists that "in order that the urge toward simpler ways of life should not lead to antisocial dreams, it must be understood once and for all that our societies will not cease to be technological unless their technical power is destroyed by unprecedented and altogether undesirable catastrophes."[40]

In contrast to the prevailing trend in the literature on the subject, however, Simon does not speculate about some assumed wholesale, abstract, ontological "impact" of technology. Rather, approaching the problem from a practical point of view, he simply looks at how technological progress actually affects specific aspects of our daily and social life. And narrowing these aspects to those he considers of particular relevance for democracy, he examines how technology has changed our views of time, nature, life, reason, labor, education, and leadership.

Simon finds our perception of time modified by the ability of technology to do things fast. In historical societies, some projects took generations to complete and thus supplied a realistic sense of continuity between the past and the future, which strengthened their community feelings. By contrast, today's ever quicker execution of most technical projects tends to isolate generations from each other. What technological power tends to do, then, according to Simon, is to deprive modern man "of a dwelling place in social duration."[41] Similarly, by changing the ratio between natural and man-made things in our environment, technology contributes also to our alienation from nature. In the context of human sentiments, Simon points out, the notion of the natural is much narrower, and the notion of the artificial much wider, than in the context of physical laws. For a chemist, a synthesized substitute is the equivalent of the natural substance. But a swimming pool, canned food, or a sunlamp can never have the same total effect on people as their natural counterparts. Technological environment affects what Simon calls our moral psychology, which is also affected by the severe reduction of the ratio of the living to the nonliving in our daily life. Pets, occasional visits to the zoo, and a Sunday drive in the countryside keep us only barely in touch with the living nature of which we are, after all, an integral part.[42] The technological rationalization of life and of life in common, Simon notes further, has also brought a radical change in our relation to *danger* and *security*. While only a few decades ago, entrusting one's life to a "flying machine" was courting death, the millions of people boarding planes today hardly give it a second thought. Similarly, today's parents worry far less than their grandparents did about a child getting sick. Science and technology have given modern societies an unprecedented sense of security regarding physical laws and environment. But as every commentator is eager to point out, there is also the other, the dark, side to this progress. Modern technology is capable, literally, of blowing up and/or poisoning the entire world. Simon does not deny it. But he puts the problem in a somewhat different perspective, which keeps it in the range of politics and free choice.

What we now dread, Simon writes, is "less and less nature and more and more man." The progress of technology has supplied our minds with patterns of unprecedented regularity and power with regard to our physical environment. We have landed on the moon and are reaching for the planets. But this spectacular success of human reason applied to deal with our physical environment is severely undermined by our inability to control also human behavior. In the ever expanding technological environment, the untrustworthiness of man is a scandal. Simon puts it this way. Human freedom, forever struggling with irresolution, perplexity, inconsistency, does not fit well with the new rationalism born of our technological power. It is not that human freedom lacks in certainty. As explained in a previous chapter, while we cannot predict what will happen next, we assert our freedom without qualification whenever, victorious over all difficulties, we choose the morally right course of action. But such superdetrmined moral choice, no less than ordinary human weaknesses and passions, may well interfere with the most feasible technical solution to a social problem. And this, of course, is not acceptable to the technological mind, for which there is no introspection, no wrenching of the soul, and indeed no freedom of choice. As Simon sees it, then, the "technological pride hates human liberty both on account of its excellence and on account of its wretchedness." And that is, in the last analysis, what makes technological ambition "the least reconcilable enemy of democracy and more generally of liberty."[43]

Turning to the question of labor and modern technology, as this was seen in his time, Simon acknowledges the usual complaints raised by humanistic writers friendly to democracy. Yes, the extreme division of labor encouraged by modern technology does not particularly help a person to develop his or her highest potential. But Simon does not see democracy at a total loss here. The introduction of the assembly line type of production, he contends, has actually helped the growth of modern democracy. This modern manufacturing method has not only made many goods cheaper but has also made it possible, for the first time in history, for the people without any special skills to earn a decent living. For Simon (and presumably for the workers involved) that opportunity offsets at least in part the discomfort and whatever intellectual deprivation may be involved in the assembly line work. For example, before the First World War, earning $5 a day at a Ford plant was a huge advancement for the many Italian and Slav immigrants, who were ready to do—and did—all kinds of far more unpleasant labor for less money.[44] Clearly, for a government of, for, and by the people it is important that the common people attain a living standard that gives them a chance to take an interest in public affairs.[45] That does not mean, of course, that all "the common people" will always take advantage of that opportunity, or that their participation will move politics in a predetermined direction. As was pointed out in the preceding chapter, universal suffrage and majority rule do not of themselves guarantee freedom and justice for all. And this is why modern technology, even as it lightens the burden of labor, will not of itself improve either the participation in or the quality of democratic politics.

Nevertheless, since contemporary industry, business, and public administration all operate with ever more sophisticated equipment, there is a steady demand for a better educated labor force, which brings concrete benefits to democratic society. Simon believes that, all things considered, to prepare citizens to participate constructively in democratic politics, the so-called humanist education is best. Acquaintance with history and the history of ideas, with theories of science as well as of politics and ethics, and with the great achievements in arts and literature is the best kind of education for individual self-government with a strong sense of social responsibility. The increasing preference for technical education, on which modern society has become so dependent for its proper operation, may therefore appear to shortchange both individual citizens and democratic society. The neglect of history, philosophy, and the arts may not cause everybody to be unhappy, but it will be inevitably reflected in social behavior and general culture. Democracy, then, has a stake in preserving humanist education. But Simon does not want to dismiss the benefits derived from the spread of technical education. The number of people who have in recent times gained access to "scientific instruction necessary for handling of techniques," he notes, is certainly greater than the number of people who have lost access to traditional humanist education. And what that means is simply that the ratio of people who receive relatively advanced types of education keeps steadily rising, which cannot be all bad for democracy.[46]

Finally, however, in considering democratic prospects in an ever more technologized physical and social environment, we must not overlook how that environment affects politics and especially political leadership. Under normal circumstances, Simon writes in his Aristotelian-Thomist idiom, "leadership belongs to prudence." When it comes to deciding what is to be done, it is far more important for leaders to be good persons—temperate, courageous, just, and prudent—than to be technical experts. But good intentions and a strong character are today hardly enough for dealing adequately with the myriad of technical problems that complicate the life of advanced modern societies, which means that democratic leaders must listen to the experts. The problem is that the technical knowledge has turned, as Simon puts it, "into an instrument so heavy as to get often out of control."[47] The increasingly daunting task of the democratic political leader, then, is to stand up for politics as "the master art."[48] The competent, prudent leader will listen to expert advice, but he must never allow his technical advisers, the economists, the generals, the physicists, to have the last word. And he faces an even more difficult political task, because as technology continues to promise a life of ease for all, he will also have to persuade the majority of the voters to prefer the just political over the most feasible technical solutions.

The dramatic advances in technology since Simon's time have plainly confirmed his evaluation of its challenge to democratic aspirations. As technological progress marches on, it has become clear to everyone that things will not work out for the best all by themselves. Experts agree that runaway technology is a threat to democracy as well as to the environment. Simon is concerned mostly with the former, and his analysis reaches to the heart of the problem. For according to Simon, what is really at stake in the conflict between democracy and technology is the choice between "the pursuit of happiness" and "the lust for power."

As Simon explains it, happiness is, of course, "the all-embracing and naturally determined object of all acts of will, and in a certain sense it is impossible to set in opposition happiness and, say, power, since no one seeks power except inasmuch as he places his happiness in it."[49] And yet, there is a sense in which restricting the pursuit of happiness to happiness is not a redundant proposition. For instance,

> of an artist who sacrfices his fortune, his health, his love, his honor, and his soul to his creation, it can be said relevantly that he has placed his happiness in his creation. But he can also relevantly reply that for the sake of his work, he has surrendered all claim to happiness. From the study of this contrast much can be learned about the meaning and conditions of harmony in human desires.[50]

The objects that fit the form of happiness, as Simon puts it, must be, first of all, *in line with human nature.* This implies willingness to accept nature such as it is, and such as we did not make it. We delude ourselves if we imagine ourselves either original creators or divinely self-sufficient. Another attribute of the objects that agree with the pursuit of happiness is their being *interior to the person.* This may be health, the feeling of being alive, even pleasure—though not of the violent kind. Works of art do not qualify any more than gold or diamonds. Next, an object fitting the form of happiness has to be *enjoyable in peace.* Thrill seekers pursuing ever new challenges for their own sake are not really looking for happiness. And last but not least, the genuine form of human happiness, according to Simon, favors especially objects capable of being *enjoyed in common.*[51]

Now modern mass societies, ever more dependent on technology, do seem to restrict the opportunity for pursuing happiness so described. The organization of modern life is busy, noisy, forever changing; it is saturated with consumer mentality; it leaves little room for the enjoyment of nature or the cultivation of lasting friendships. American population is listed as 95 percent urban, and the average citizen changes residence three times in his or her lifetime; only one in eight American citizens dies in the same locality in which he or she was born; and one in three marriages in America ends in divorce. The Jeffersonian myth of rural democracy of independent farmers may still be invoked on patriotic occasions, but its nostalgic appeal is waning. Realistically speaking, the ideal of a happy life on the family farm is no match for the temptations of an ever more technological lifestyle. Thus in speculating about the future, Simon writes, "a general return to primitive conditions is the most unreal of all constructs." Technology is here to stay and to develop further.[52] And that means that friends of democracy must keep up "a program of never ending inquiry into difficulties which cannot disappear but can be defined with more and more precision."[53]

BEYOND CAPITALISM AND TECHNOLOGY

The widening of the gap between the rich and the poor and the destruction of the natural environment are two good examples of certain tendencies of capitalism and technology for which contemporary democracy has yet to find appropriate solutions. But we need also to recognize that, precisely as a community of the free, democracy has other problems as well. Thus even if both capitalism and technology were to be brought under effective democratic control, this does not mean that democracy's worries would be over. For like any other regime, democracy has built-in problems of its own, independent from external circumstances. Two famous historical critiques of democracy will illustrate this point. They were proposed long before either capitalism or technology, as we know them, had became established, and yet they describe vividly conditions familiar to our own experience. The more recent of these critiques anticipates the specifically modern temptations of mass democracy. But the other, more than two thousand years old, points to its generic weakness and deserves to be recalled first.

Democratic society and the democratic personality excite nothing but contempt from Plato, and he excoriates them both mercilessly. But the sad truth is, of course, that even after two millennia and under radically different conditions, his criticism has by no means lost all of its sting. What makes democracy especially appealing, Plato quotes Socrates as saying, is that it tolerates and encourages diversity. But Socrates is being sarcastic. He sees this democratic diversity, i.e., freedom and equality, marching in "a splendid garlanded procession of insolence, license, extravagance, and shamelessness," which have been renamed respectively good breeding, liberty, generosity, and courage. In democracy, there is no compulsion either to exercise authority which one may have, or to submit to any authority, if one does not want to. In democracy, one may well run into convicted criminals in the street. Democracy does not care about the character of its politicians, as long as they profess themselves people's friends. In democracy, all pleasures have equal rights, and no distinction is made between necessary and unnecessary desires. And so, according to Socrates, because they glorify "liberty and equality without order or restraint," the people in democracy eventually lose all ability to resist either pain or pleasure. Democracy dissolves into anarchy and is succeeded by tyranny.[54]

Something like that reportedly happened more than once in ancient Greek history, and the sequence may even explain in part what happened in Germany early in the twentieth century. Contemporary democracy, however, faces a somewhat different threat. Peering into the future 175 years ago, Tocqueville had no name for it, but his description allows us to recognize the problem as real and present. Beholding a huge mass of individuals, all equal and alike, Tocqueville, like Plato, sees them obsessed with their own "petty and paltry pleasures." But in contrast to Plato's version of what happens next, Tocqueville does not see these democratic masses necessarily threatened by takeover by mean mad tyrants. He envisages for them conceivably an even worse possible fate. "Above this race of men," Tocqueville writes, "stands an immense and tutelary power, which takes upon itself alone to secure their gratification and watch over their fate." "Absolute, minute, regular, and provident," this power is by no means harsh or cruel. On the contrary, its image is reminiscent of the rule of Plato's philosopher-king, under which the people are well taken care of even though they have no political rights whatsoever. Tocqueville does not know whether this will come to pass, but "more commonly than it is believed," he writes, this corruption of democracy could well be combined with some "outer forms of freedom under the wing of the sovereignty of the people."[55]

The enduring relevance of these historic critiques of democracy is presently confirmed in the liberal/communitarian exchanges about the direction American democracy may be heading. With only occasional references to capitalism and technology in faint background, this debate in effect borrows its charges from Plato and Tocqueville. What do the two sides reproach each other respectively? The liberal defense of the priority of individual rights, including both "necessary and unnecessary desires," as it were, recalls for the communitarians precisely what Plato said was wrong with democracy and would lead to its demise. At the same time, however, the communitarians' emphasis on the need for a sovereign democratic authority raises for the liberals the specter of that absolute power that Tocqueville feared could "prevent individual existence" even in a formal democracy. Or to put it another way, the liberals accuse the communitarians of praising conformism, while the communitarians see the liberals flirting with anarchy. A closer look at these allegations, however, reveals that the two sides actually agree on what makes for true democracy. In defense of their own positions, the liberals and the communitarians both reject Plato's caricature of as well as Tocqueville's fears for democracy. And solidly in Tocqueville's camp, they all want his hopes, not his fears, to come true.

Let us, then, acknowledge that, transcending problems with both capitalism and technology, the real test for democracy is to be found in the quality of its citizens' self-government. One does not have to deny that external circumstances and specific institutional arrangements may either help or hinder the fulfillment of basic democratic aspirations. Democracy might perhaps have a better chance of being practiced in a small rural than in a large urban industrial society, but that is by no means guaranteed. What the enemies of democracy have forever argued is that regardless of circumstances, democracy discourages the pursuit of excellence, defends mediocrity, alternately favors anarchy and conformity, and is helpless to prevent society's eventual descent into barbarism. And looking at what is going on in democratic societies today, honest democrats will themselves acknowledge the germ of truth in these charges. But what they must not do, is to blame those problems on capitalism and technology alone. Would effective control over both technology and capitalism solve all of democracy's problems? Or would not equal justice and opulence for all bring it rather face-to-face with its ultimate problem, namely, the quality of its citizens' self-government?

The ancient royal and aristocratic regimes are today condemned not only for having shamelessly exploited the common people but also for the extravagant and corrupt lifestyle often indulged by their rulers. The aristocracy-aping capitalist bourgeoisie of early modern history is open to the same double charge. But what is to prevent the victorious masses themselves, exploiting the potential of modern technology, from adopting the lifestyle of the former ruling classes? Is there anything that could help the community of the free, the equal, and now also the well-off to avoid being corrupted by its historical success?

NOTES

1. Taking a quick tour around the globe, Thomas Carothers attributes these disparities to "retrenchment." See his "Democracy Without Illusions," *Foreign Affairs*, 76:1 (January/February 1997), pp. 85–99. For a thoughtful comment on the mood in the United States, see Michael J. Sandel, *Democracy's Discontent: America in Search of a Public Philosophy* (Cambridge: Belknap Press, 1996).

2. *Democracy in America*, vol. 1, p. ix.

3. See Michael Novak, *The Spirit of Democratic Capitalism* (New York: American Enterprise Institute, 1986), "Introduction: Capitalism, Socialism, and Religion—An Inquiry into the Spiritual Wealth of Nations."

4. *The Habits of the Heart*, ed. Robert N. Bellah et al. (Berkeley, CA: University of California Press, 1996).

5. Samuel Bowles and Herbert Gintis, *Democracy and Capitalism: Property, Community, and the Contradictions of Modern Social Thought* (New York: Basic Books, 1986), p. 209.

6. Ibid., p. 118.

7. Ibid., p. 71.

8. Ibid., p. 65.

9. Ibid., p. 25.

10. Ibid., p. 176.

11. Yves R. Simon, *The Philosophy of Democratic Government* (Chicago: University of Chicago Press, 1951), p. 248.

12. Conceding that his terms "beg questions," Simon calls these stages "democratic" and "socialistic." The first stage began in the late eighteenth century, and it may be considered over, at least in the leading Western countries. The second, which began around the middle of the nineteenth century, has still a long ways to go. *Democratic Government*, p. 233.

13. *Work, Society, and Culture*, p. 96. See also John Plamenatz, *The Revolutionary Movement in France, 1815–1871* (London: Longmans, Green, 1952).

14. Michael Novak denies that the term "invisible hand" is intended to mystify the operation of the market. He calls it a mere metaphor and points out that it appears only twice in the nine hundred pages of *The Wealth of Nations*. Novak writes: "The metaphor, simply put, draws attention to unintended consequences. The *motives* of individuals, it suggests, are not the same as the *social consequences* of their actions. The logic of economic behavior lies on a plane different from that of the logic of motives." *Democratic Capitalism*, p. 114. But even if true, that interpretation in no way supports Novak's principal claim that private profit motives necessarily produce beneficial social consequences. What is quite certain, however, is that democratic political victories cannot be explained as unintended consequences of capitalist private enterprise.

15. Yves R. Simon, *The Community of the Free* (New York: Henry Holt, 1947), p. 153.

16. For the latest complaint about money as the curse of democratic politics, see Ronald Dworkin, *Freedom's Law* (Cambridge, MA: Harvard University Press, 1996). See also *Paying for Presidents* (New York: Twentieth Century Fund, 1993).

17. *Community of the Free*, p. 155.

18. Ibid., p. 157.

19. Ibid., p. 159.

20. *Ethics*, Bk 5, ch. 5. Aristotle calls the rule of equality in exchanges among citizens commutative justice. But as he expects the community to interfere when this rule is violated, for example, when contracts are not lived up to, Aristotle calls it also corrective justice. Simon wishes Aristotle had done a better job of explaining his terms. See Yves R. Simon, *The Definition of Moral Virtue* (New York: Fordham University Press, 1986, 1989), pp. 99–100.

21. *Democratic Government*, p. 236.

22. *Work, Society, and Culture*, p. 137.

23. *Community of the Free*, p. 169; *Democratic Government*, p. 257.

24. David Ricardo, *Principles of Political Economy* (1817), quoted in George H. Sabine, *A History of Political Theory* (New York: Holt, Reinhart and Winston, 1961), p. 692.

25. *Democratic Government*, p. 250. In its annual survey of "What People Earn?" the Sunday supplement magazine *Parade* of June 12, 1998, lists at random the $66 million income of a popular TV entertainer between the incomes of two ordinary people with incomes in the twenty- to thirty-thousand-dollar range.

26. *Community of the Free*, p. 172.

27. See Edward N. Wolff, *Top Heavy: The Increasing Inequality of Wealth in America and What Can Be Done about It* (New York: Twentieth Century Fund, 1996), p. 11. Additional disturbing statistics: Ranked by "household wealth," the top 1 percent of the population in the United States owned 39 percent of

the country's wealth in 1989, compared to 26 percent for the top 1 percent in France, 25 in Canada, 18 in Great Britain, and 16 in Sweden. Edward N. Wolff, "How the Pie is Sliced: America's Growing Concentration of Wealth," in *Ticking Time Bombs: The New Conservative Assault on Democracy,* ed. Robert L. Kuttner (New York: New Press, 1996), p. 76.

28. The globalization of capitalist economics is making the situation worse by undoing some of the hard-won achievements of the democratic labor movements. Because "democratic capitalism" can now look for maximum profit opportunities anywhere on earth, labor in democratic countries has lost some of its bargaining power. See for instance, Dani Rodrick, *Has Globalization Gone Too Far?* (Cambridge, MA: Harvard University Press, 1996). This subject cannot be pursued here, but the following, not atypical, example shows what is happening in the world at large. The Nike corporation paid an average female worker making its athletic shoes in Indonesia approximately $0.82 a day in 1991, and it paid Michael Jordan $20 million to advertise those shoes, the latter amount being greater than all the wages paid to all the workers who produced the shoes. See Richard Barnet and John Cavanaugh, *Global Dreams: Imperial Corporations and the New World Order* (New York: Simon and Schuster, 1994), pp. 326–28.

29. According to news reports, by exercising his stock options, the CEO of the Walt Disney enterprises raised his compensation for 1997 to more than $500 million. On a previous occasion, he had collected $200 million. And another Disney executive was given $90 million in compensation after being fired. At this writing, the "worth" of "the richest man in the world," Bill Gates, is about to top $50 trillion.

30. Yves R. Simon, *The Tradition of Natural Law* (New York: Fordham University Press, 1965, 1992), p. 165. Health care seems the preferred target of the opponents of "the welfare state" but some of their arguments are less than convincing. For instance, Richard A. Epstein argues that the best health service can only be provided by strictly private enterprise. Yet even while advising against "public expressions of compassion," he suggests that perhaps doctors could take off a few hours from their regular practice to give medical help for the poor "at a storefront run by a local church or neighborhood group." See his *Mortal Peril: Our Inalienable Right to Health Care?* (New York: Addison-Wesley, 1997), p. 324. Similarly, Regina Herzlinger contends that "only the market can provide the health care that the American people want at a price they are willing to pay." But the standard example she uses in discussing the financial aspects of health care is "a family making $100,00 a year." And to illustrate how the notion of fully informed buyers applies to the health care market, she cites the example of a woman who "custom designed the types of incisions that removed her breast cancer tumor, faxed questions that arose from her research about cancer to her surgeons, and even selected classical music to be played in the operating room."

In *Market-Driven Health Care: Who Wins, Who Loses in the Transformation of America's Largest Service Industry* (New York: Addison-Wesley, 1997). See also Andrew Hacker's review of both these books in *The New York Review*, June 12, 1997, pp. 26–28.

31. *Democratic Government*, p. 245.

32. *Work, Society, and Culture*, p. 124.

33. The literature on the problem of technology is vast and rapidly expanding. A thoughful recent volume is *Technology in the Western Political Tradition*, ed. A. M. Melzer, J. Weinberger, and M. R. Zinman (Ithaca, NY: Cornell University Press, 1993). This collection of essays was gathered at the Symposium on Science, Reason, and Modern Democracy, founded in 1989 at the Michigan State University.

34. See Reiner Schürmann, "Technicity, Topology, Tragedy: Heidegger on That Which 'Saves,' " in *Technology in the Western Political Tradition*, ch. 8. The editors of this collection summarize Schürmann's interpretation as follows: Technology saves "by way of technological nihilism, which discloses the complete uniqueness of the technological epoch and thus the utter singularity of Being, which always strives against and ruptures every attempt of technological reason to construct universal norms and standards. Technological nihilism saves by readying us to embrace the tragic contingency of every foundation and construction (such as a conception of justice, an edifice of instrumental reason, or community of philosophy, or political deliberation), and by allowing us to see that this tragedy is never ours, but belongs rather to the singular happening of Being." P. xii. Heidegger's "The Question Concerning Technology," is included in *The Question Concerning Technology and Other Essays*, trans. W. Lowitt (New York: Harper, 1977).

35. See Gianni Vattimo, "Postmodernity, Technology, Ontology," in *Technology in the Western Political Tradition*, ch. 9.

36. See chapter 3 above.

37. The three last chapters of *Technology in the Western Political Tradition* summarize nicely the difficulties involved in treating this subject. "Liberal Democracy and the Problem of Technology," by William A. Galston, is followed by "Technology and the Problem of Liberal Democracy," by Jerry Weinberger, leading to the concluding comments on "The Problem with the 'Problem of Technology,' " by Arthur M. Melzer. But see also Richard E. Sclove, *Democracy and Technology* (New York: Guilford Press, 1995). Eschewing philosophical speculation, the book includes a thirty-three page bibliography of recent writings on technology, and a note on the Loka Institute, founded at Amherst in 1987, "dedicated to making science and technology more responsive to democratically decided social and environmental concerns."

38. *Democratic Government*, p. 261.

39. Ibid., p. 267. Simon elaborates on the general notion of use also in *Practical Knowledge*, pp. 51–61, and in *Definition of Moral Virtue*, pp. 19–29.

40. *Democratic Government*. p. 273.

41. Ibid., p. 275.

42. Ibid., p. 277.

43. Ibid., p. 278.

44. *Work, Society, and Culture*, p. 167.

45. Whether the transfer of Western technologies to the many so-called underdeveloped countries will have the same effect on their politics is by no means clear. The Western experience has been decisively shaped also by the native liberal democratic ideology. In the rest of the world, the self-evidence of political liberty and equality is mostly an imported truth.

46. *Democratic Government*, p. 279.

47. Ibid.

48. "Since politics uses the rest of the sciences, and since, again, it legislates what we are to do and what we are to abstain from, the end of this science must include those of the others, so that this end must be the good for man." *Ethics* 1.1. 1094^b, 5–9.

49. *Democratic Government*, p. 262.

50. *Freedom of Choice*, pp. 45–46. For instance, Nietzsche places the happiness of his superman in his art. Sitting on a stone before his cave, Zarathustra answers his animals' query: "I ceased long ago to strive for my happiness: I strive for my work." *Democratic Government*, p. 262.

51. *Democratic Government*, p. 266. Simon finds Rousseau's view of happiness hopelessly misleading, precisely because it ignores the first and the last of these conditions. Relaxing at the bottom of a drifting boat, Rousseau talks to himself: "What is it that one enjoys in such a situation? Nothing external to one's self; nothing, except one's self and one's own existence; so long as this state endures, one is, like God, self-sufficient." Ibid., p. 265. (Quoted from *Rêveries du promeneur solitaire*.)

52. It is unreasonable to oppose technology, Simon writes on his last page, but "it is not unreasonable to consider that a small number of lofty souls can give the family farm, in our time, a historical and, as it were, transcendent meaning." And what the example of these people would affirm for all to see, according to Simon, are "things that can never become indifferent to men: communion with universal nature, the conquest of time through everlasting faithfulness, temperance, dignity in poverty, holy leisure, contemplation." *Democratic Government*, p. 322.

53. Ibid., p. 319.

54. Plato, *Republic*, pp. 556–62.

55. *Democracy in America*, vol. 2, pp. 336–37.

6

DEMOCRACY'S CHOICES

Democratic politics may be lagging behind the expansion of capitalism and technology, but the political enfranchisement of the masses is likely to continue. For even if not everyone is fully convinced that all are born free and equal, the appeal of democratic freedom and equality, once proposed on the worldwide scale, cannot be easily withdrawn. So the preferences of the ordinary people not just in politics but in every aspect of social life are likely to be considered ever more attentively by those in charge. In fact, public opinion and consumer demand are already what public officials and corporate executives alike worry about. It is a pity that democrats do not worry about it more.

With the rising living standards and the reduction of the workloads for most people, the style of life in democratic societies will increasingly be determined by how the ordinary people choose to occupy their leisure time. In the past, leisure was the privilege of only a few in any society who, free from want and labor, were in charge of both the government and cultural activities. But today this privilege, qualified as it may be, has been extended from the few to the many who are now asserting it in the cultural no less than in the political life of democratic societies. And judging by the record, the prospects are not altogether encouraging. Clearly, democratic political victories do not automatically guarantee also cultural progress.

This is not a simple problem. If we take "culture" in its narrower sense as representing "intellectual and moral improvement" and "what is regarded as excellent in arts, letters, manners, scholarly pursuits, etc.," democratic countries today are clearly the most cultured in the world. They are ahead in science, philosophy, art, humane politics, and perhaps even in personal morals. But if we take "culture" in the broader sense used by anthropologists, which includes everything people do, the picture changes somewhat. For example, the way many people spend their leisure time in the United States, the prototypical technologically advanced democratic country, helps the term "popular culture" to retain its dismissive connotation. And it will not do to argue that discriminating among popular preferences is undemocratic. Modern democracy is supposed to disprove, not confirm, Plato's caricature of the regime.

To put the risks of a popular democratic culture in historical perspective, we need to recall that the so-called ruling and leisure classes in traditional societies had throughout history also spent a good part of their wealth and freedom from labor in activities that had little to do with their or anyone else's intellectual and moral improvement. Still, because the overwhelming majority of the people were preoccupied with just making a living, these aberrations by the few had only limited consequences for the overall operation of society.[1] But that is no longer the case. With so many people now enjoying a fair standard of living, a good deal of free time, and access to sophisticated technologies, the waste and abuse of leisure can today take place on an unprecedented society-wide scale. In fact, new complaints are daily heard about the shoddiness of "popular culture," and not a few TV programs, movies, bestseller books, musical genres, theme parks, sporting competitions, recreational pastimes, commercial advertisements, and last but not least, political campaigns and commentary lend themselves as illustrations for the coarsening of tastes, attitudes, and behavior.

Trying to address and sort out these specific complaints, however, does not lead far, because arguments in defense of democratic freedom and equality for all block any closure at that level. To take a single example, it is doubtful that anything anyone could say against it would dissuade the millions of people who watch "professional" wrestling on TV for hours on end and are more than willing to pay to attend live performances, so that they, too, might have a chance to clown for the camera. And what is more, many people who may actually despise such spectacles are still likely to tell critics to "lighten up." They will use political arguments against censorship and will defend attendance at these or similar events as the people's free choice and inalienable right, perhaps also adding that their staging is, after all, legitimate free enterprise. Clearly, then, to evaluate the chances of continuing democratic progress, cultural as well as political, the problem needs to be approached from a different perspective.

In what follows, I propose to establish such a perspective relying on Simon's analysis of the meaning of work and its role in individual and social life, in politics and culture. Things have changed radically since the famous Dr. Johnson confidently declared that "all intellectual improvement arises from leisure; and all leisure arises from one working for another." As long as the masses labored from dawn to dusk, the connection between politics and culture, on the one hand, and freedom from want and labor, on the other hand, was plain for all to see. But that connection is not so obvious today. The progressive distribution of leisure among ever more people, who now have also some disposable wealth, has produced rather mixed results, as noted above. We are not sure that leisure is the true basis of culture, and we need to clarify the relation of work to politics. As the tile of a collection of essays addressing the new situation asked anxiously a generation ago, *Leisure: A Blessing or a Curse?*[2] It is a good guess that "killing time" is a modern expression. But we need to sample other opinions.

LEISURE AND CULTURE

In a massive study, *Of Time, Work, and Leisure*, Sebastian de Grazia combines detailed sociological research of the problem with some side comments on democratic politics and culture. Thus, to begin with, de Grazia wonders whether time spent at work has really been reduced as much as it is believed. Though people may no longer work twelve hours a day, seven days a week in mills and mines and factories, or farms, the current forty-hour workweek seems hardly an accurate measure of time devoted to work by most people. For one thing, commuting to work today may often take hours. And for another, the extra money people want to spend on that guaranteed annual vacation they usually earn by working overtime during the year. In fact, statistics show that in the countries with the shortest nominal workweek, part-time and even full-time moonlighting is steadily rising. De Grazia also wonders whether time spent in union activities, or job-related community action and politics, can be counted as "free time." And what about all those self-improvement and training courses, he asks, taken in order to qualify for a better job, which is desired presumably because it promises not just more pay but more "free time"? To de Grazia, all this appears absurd and hopeless. "We have transformed civilization and our lives," he writes, "to win time and find leisure, but we have failed. . . . [W]e have raised a range of Himalayan institutions and habits that block our way forward or backward."[3]

De Grazia does not think that the majority of mankind is capable of true leisure, and consequently he divides people into two types: those who love ideas and the imagination, and the great majority who do not particularly care for either. The first group creates and transmits high culture; the members of the majority are perfectly satisfied with avoiding that culture. And all things considered, de Grazia thinks this is all for the best. Sometimes, he writes,

> it is as hard to convince people that everybody does not want leisure as it is to convince them that in the days of domestics, servants pitied their masters' lot. Much of Plato's *Republic* is devoted to the simple proposition that we cannot all be philosophers. And if we can't be philosophers, we'd be bored with leisure.[4]

Because they include work with their principle of equality, democratic and socialist ideologies, according to de Grazia, are both undermining cultured leisure. Some sort of equality is recognized, he writes, under all forms of government and in all religions, e.g., the equality of being a member of that state or of that church. Different ideologies take it from there and prescribe other equalities "before the law of God or man." But both democracy and socialism insist on combining the doctrine of equality with

> the universal duty of work (or the paradoxical "right" to it) . . . thereby making everybody not alone a worker but a beneficiary of free time as well. All workers get it . . . and no one has a right to more of it than others. The distribution of free time thus cannot change without a change in the doctrine of work and equality.[5]

This change, de Grazia claims, can only come about on the initiative of individuals whom he calls "the leisure kind." Those who appreciate ideas and imagination, he argues, will simply have to persuade the masses that this world is not just to be mastered but also marveled at.

In fact, de Grazia contends that if those who are bored by culture are free to leave it alone, those interested in culture should in turn be exempted from democratic "work duty."[6] How such a division of society into culture lovers and the rest of the people might affect democratic practice and aspirations, de Grazia does not say. But even if what he suggests be no more than a division of labor, de Grazia sometimes reads as if he endorses Dr. Johnson's formula for culture, which requires "one working for another."

Another, and different, interpretation of leisure is offered by sociologist Chris Rojek, employing what he claims to be the latest methodology developed in his discipline. Thus rather than as some alleged freedom from work, Rojek defines leisure as "relations of permissible behavior," which are determined by the "structural rules of pleasure and unpleasure," in a "historically structured economy of leisure."[7] And he traces that historically structured development of leisure in the modern era in three overlapping stages.[8] Under capitalism, he explains, leisure has been turned into a salable commodity, and any protests against its "commodification" tend to be "reabsorbed" by the market. At the same time, however, seeing its early hopes for mastering history frustrated by actual events, "the spirit of modernity" (embracing technology and democracy) has turned cynical and now denounces "leisure industry as tireless impresario dedicated to the cult of distraction" with which to fill "the consumers' empty time." But finally, as if reacting against this defeatism, postmodern interpreters of leisure, according to Rojek, actually welcome the blurring of the distinctions between culture and commerce, work and leisure, performer and audience, writer and reader, etc., which they see as an integral and positive aspect of "existence without commitment." In fact, the "virtual reality" provided by the "multiphrenic intensity" of "telematic technology," Rojek writes, is the perfect match for the "language game" reality of postmodern philosophy. Rojek admits that all these things remain rather in flux, but he nevertheless wants to suggest in conclusion that the postmodern "decentering leisure" could well serve to dispel the modern illusion that saw leisure primarily as freedom and escape.[9]

Finally, for a third sample of contemporary views we may turn to a writer who manages to praise leisure without setting it in opposition to either work or democracy. As Joseph Pieper explains it, even though it differs from work in some fundamental respects, leisure is itself an active condition and there is no reason why anyone should be barred from it. In his somewhat metaphorical style, Pieper describes work as being mostly noise, toil, and utility. By contrast, leisure is a silent but active listening to the mystery of the world that includes being at peace with oneself and with the world. Indeed, without this double affirmation, not working means simply being idle and could well presage sliding into sloth. But finally, we must also understand that, in contrast to work, true leisure rises above utility. Leisure, Pieper writes, "does not exist for the sake of work—however much strength it may give a man to work." Its justification is not as either mental or physical restorative. The point of leisure is not that the worker should do better work but rather that he should "be capable of seeing life as a whole and the world as a whole."[10]

Like de Grazia and Rojek, Pieper acknowledges that the meanings of both leisure and work are closely tied with ideology and politics, and this makes him, too, somewhat apprehensive about the prospect of realizing the "hopes of leisure" in modern democratic society. For him, work is a necessary and a good thing, but he deplores the social pressures that want people "fettered to the process of work," as if work were all there was to human existence. Thus Pieper believes that the democratic society must give all who work for a living an opportunity both to acquire property and to enrich their inner lives. And in his opinion, this could well be achieved simply by paying everyone honest wages and providing all with a decent education.[11]

It is this last requirement especially that makes one wonder about the choice of Pieper's English title, *Leisure: The Basis of Culture*. In order to "deproletarize," as he puts it, modern society, it is by no means enough merely to redress the injustices of the capitalist distribution of wealth. To break the fetters of the process of work and to be able to enjoy leisure, a person needs activities worth engaging in for their own sake. In the Middle Ages, these activities were called *artes liberales*, in contrast to *artes serviles* that are always pursued for the sake of something else. Thus the access to leisure, Pieper writes,

> cannot be provided by purely political measures . . . by "freeing" the
> life of the individual economically. Although this would entail much
> that is necessary, the *essential* would still be wanting. The provision of
> an external opportunity for leisure is not enough; it can only be fruit-
> ful if the man himself is capable of leisure and can, as we say, "occupy

his leisure," or (as the Greeks still more clearly say) *skolen agein,* "work his leisure" (this usage brings out very clearly the by no means "leisurely" character of leisure).[12]

We need to pause here to acknowledge the full import of what Pieper is saying. For his account represents a decisive correction to the historical-ideological misunderstandings of the true relations, on the one hand, between leisure and culture, and on the other hand, between culture and work. Approaching the question of leisure from a philosophical rather than a sociological point of view, Pieper reveals what once pointed out should be clear to all: leisure requires culture, and culture requires work. Samuel Johnson may have described fairly the situation as it appeared to his eighteenth-century peers. But to say that "all intellectual improvement arises from leisure [and] all leisure arises from one working for another" is simply false. Just being relieved from working for a living will make no one wise. Having time to spend is neutral between boredom and leisure. To enjoy true leisure, one has to acquire some culture to occupy it with. Thus what Pieper affirms and insists on in his exposition is the exact opposite of what his title, perpetuating the confusion of names, announces. Culture is the basis of leisure, not the other way around.[13]

Now if we call leisure the time left after biologically necessary functions and duties have been fulfilled, we need leisure for work every bit as much as for culture.[14] But if leisure is understood as Pieper describes it, namely, an excellent active human condition that rises above utility, that condition clearly depends on "liberal arts," or culture, to sustain it. Thus the objective order among human activities, spanning the range from necessity to freedom, and from survival to fulfillment, is represented by the following sequence: Work, culture, leisure. In the present context, let us also add that the democratic pursuit of happiness is not exempt from this chronological existential order. Democratic culture cannot be anything else but work in progress. And as we shall see in conclusion, that rule applies definitely also to democracy itself.

CULTURE AND WORK

What Pieper's title, *Leisure: The Basis of Culture,* fairly describes is the sharp contrast between the life of work and the life of culture which dominates opinion in what Simon calls "the classical societies." Simon admits that "classical" is a rather vague term, but he is satisfied that the opposition between culture and work is one of its characteristic features. For example, in contrast to the times of Homer, when the king's daughter does the laundry with her maids, any manual work becomes for Plato "mean employment lacking in higher principles," while Aristotle suggests that laborers work "as fire burns," that is, by sheer habit without thought.[15] Indeed, according to Plutarch, no person of noble birth would even want to be Phidias. A gentleman may enjoy contemplating the sculptor's masterpieces, but he would never use hammer and chisel and get covered with sweat and dust.[16] Similar attitudes prevailed in classical Rome, but Simon moves on to the seventeenth century, where Pascal (1623–1662) scoffs at those who present Plato and Aristotle as what we might today call academic workers ("dressed in the gown of pedantic people"). For Pascal, Plato and Aristotle are aristocratic gentlemen (*honnêtes hommes*) who bear their philosophy lightly and do not have to "work" at it. And according to Simon, Leibnitz (1664–1716), too, writes philosophy so that society people can follow it without having to bother with technical scientific terms. In short, in the classical societies what philosophers, scientists, statesmen, and literary people did was simply not considered "work."[17]

By contrast, today we speak of social work, artistic work, and intellectual work, in addition to technical work, medical work, psychiatric work, and educational work, not to mention legal work, administrative work, scientific work, and indeed cultural work. This change in usage clearly has something to do with the fact that after being excluded from society as slaves, serfs, indentured servants, and hired hands for most of history, the people who "turn things to human use" have in modern time become full-fledged citizens. They are now, as Simon puts it, all "*social* workers."[18] The extension of the meaning of work, then, which now covers practically anything people do, owes much to the victory of democratic ideology over traditional opinions. But that does not exclude the possibility that the radically changed conditions of modern life, mixing technology, capitalism, and democratic politics, have in fact opened a clearer view onto the nature of work and its role in society. Simon has no doubts about it. The modern usage represents to him a vast improvement upon historical understanding of the meaning of work. Intellectual work, technical work, social work, etc., he holds, are all correctly called work. And proving himself once again an independent and original thinker, Simon establishes his position on the basis of Aristotle's theory of culture.[19]

In book six of *Ethics*, Aristotle discusses five so-called "intellectual virtues," to wit, understanding, science, wisdom, art, and prudence, which he proposes as the foundation or framework of culture. Simon prefers to call these qualities habitus, rather than virtues, and to make it simpler, he sets aside "understanding" (*nous*), which he deems a natural quality, and he includes "wisdom" (*sophia*) with science.[20] This leaves him with science (*episteme*), which sets our mind at ease in the field of demonstrable conclusions; art (*techne*), which enables us to deal with things to be made; and prudence (*phronesis*), which makes us confident with regard to what has to be done. The effort needed to acquire these qualities Aristotle invariably calls practice, but Simon does not hesitate to call it also work. No one can become a scientist, or an artisan/artist, or a prudent person without working hard for it. Moreover, even though science, art, and prudence, once acquired, constitute the most intimate, personal (immanent) qualities, that is clearly not the end of the story. Since these qualities can only be proven in practice, not only their attainment but their exercise, too, is a kind of work. In fact, we all take science, art, and prudence to be the foundation of culture. But according to Simon, to be fully appreciated as standards of cultural achievement, science, art, and prudence need to be recognized specifically as intellectual, technical, and social work.

THE WORKS OF THE MIND

To define "work," Simon takes its most obvious case, namely, manual work. Everyone agrees that, say, making a chair is work, and its main characteristics are easy to spot. Dealing with physical nature, directly or with tools, manual work is first of all a transitive activity: its principal effect is external to the agent. Second, manual work is a rational activity: the worker knows he is making a chair. Third, manual work is an activity by way of change: when the chair is made, the work is over and done. A realistic definition of work, however, is not complete without its fourth and fifth components, which turn out to be in fact its most recognizable features. Thus, whereas work must always be done in accordance with "the law of what is," in order to be acknowledged as work, an activity must also be socially useful. For instance, while artists may paint castles in the sky, workers cannot modify the law of gravity; building a model ship in a bottle may look like work, but it is only a hobby; and burglars about to crack a safe are not working—they are committing a crime.[21]

With appropriate qualifications, these characteristics of manual work are found also in "the works of the mind," of which, as indicated above, Simon distinguishes three kinds: technical, social, and intellectual.[22] These works of the mind are all rational, transitive, socially useful activities aimed respectively at bringing change in nature, in society, and in knowledge itself. Thus architects and engineers planning and directing manual labor, say, in building bridges and canals and draining marshes, are engaged in technical work. Social work, in turn, is done not only by those who are today officially classified as "welfare workers" but also by teachers, judges, magistrates, policemen, soldiers, and political actors, all of whom are needed to keep society going. But finally, there is also the work of the mind that does not aim either at the transformation of physical nature or at the adjustment of social relations, except incidentally. Intellectual work is a rational activity by way of change that aims at its own improvement. We engage in intellectual work to learn the truth not only about the world and its content in which we are included but specifically also about how intellectual work itself is done. Simon insists that, as the eye is made for apprehending colors, whether or not it always sees them correctly, our knowing faculty is made for truth.[23]

Today, science is glorified mostly on account of the unprecedented power it has placed in our hands to manipulate not only the physical world but also social relations. But what does this proven power reveal, if not that at least some of the knowledge behind it must, in some relevant, objective sense, be *true*? Scientific knowledge is today mankind's most useful, most pragmatic tool, and there is nothing wrong in saying that truth is what works. Thus all intellectual work is practical, rational, transitive activity by way of change. But if our research ignores "the law of what is," we cannot expect it to "pay off." The powers of the mind have many uses in the transforming of nature, in the organizing of society, and indeed in the improving of knowledge itself. But "the discourse of reason" has also its own distinct aim. Simon writes:

Technical thinking is a work of the mind which is not ultimately concerned with a state of the mind but with a condition to be brought about in physical nature. Moral work, the work of ethical wisdom, is a work of the mind which is not ultimately concerned with a state of the mind but with a state of the appetites, of the desires, of the wills of men. But the last, and in all respects the highest, kind of intellectual work is concerned with the possession of truth.[24]

For Simon, then, a worthy, genuinely humanist culture will have to have truth for its ideal aim. "Let the knowledge of truth," he writes, "not the possession of culture, be our regulating ideal. And let us not doubt that, if truth is sought according to its own laws and to its own spirit, culture also will be attained."[25] And so will also the state of leisure as described by Pieper. For once we grasp even the slightest truth, which may take us years of research, we can indeed stop and rest. As Simon explains that condition, "we are not inactive, yet our activity is not by way of change; it is motionless, it is eternity."[26] In possession of truth, we are truly at Pieper's leisure, "listening to the mystery of the world." But committed as Simon is to the priority of contemplation, he does not get carried away with its praises. For the corresponding existential truth of the matter is that no one can be at rest for very long, and no society can be composed exclusively of contemplatives. People have other things that they must do, as does society. And there is always more truth to be discovered by hard intellectual work.

A realistic model of cultural progress, then, is an ascending spiral repeating our previously established sequence of work, culture, leisure. But one problem remains. If the possession of truth is that exalted state above utility, motion, and time, as Pieper claims, how exactly can it be attained by work, which is by definition useful, transitive activity by way of change? In a general way, everyone understands that culture is supported by intellectual, technical, and social work. But how exactly can that work-produced culture blossom out, as it were, into activities pursued freely at leisure for their own sake? Is there a way for the intellectual, technical, and social works of the mind, or any of them, to transcend necessity and "the law of what is," to expand into realities of their own making that are fit to "occupy" genuine leisure?

Here we shall leave aside the more technical treatment of this subject in favor of the examples Simon offers to show how different kinds of work may transcend what he calls "legal fulfillment" and become activities of "free development."[27] Thus, while philosophical search for truth may be too "metaphysical" for some, most people will accept mathematics as a distinguished exemplar of intellectual work. And so Simon points to the developments in modern mathematics, and symbolic logic, as particularly striking illustrations of how science, that is, intellectual work that puts us at ease in the domain of demonstrable conclusions, can transcend objective, physical necessity for truths of its own making. In contrast to their historical utilitarian understanding, modern developments in both these disciplines, Simon points out, have been mostly "in the nature of free expansion rather than in the nature of legal fulfillment." Not much of this new mathematics and logic has any practical use, but this only proves that "when the scientific mind has nothing else to do but search for truth, there is for it an escape into luxury, extravagance, plenitude—yes, even infinity." And Simon guesses that this possibility is not limited to logic and mathematics but is present in all science.[28] In other words, looking for an activity with which to occupy our leisure for an occasional glimpse of eternity and infinity, we can hardly do better than engage in intellectual work.

With regard to the technical work of the mind, Aristotle's *techne* that renders us at ease with regard to things to be made, Simon remains on more familiar ground when he proposes that things to be made can escape necessity by being made beautiful. His classical example is the scene from Plato's *Symposium*, where at the end of the feast, large trays of fruit are brought before the guests who, fully satiated, can only admire the beauty of their arrangement. According to Simon, this scene shows how the technical work of the mind, even though bound strictly by the givens of physical nature, can also produce its own, *beautiful* reality, whose contemplation lifts us above desire as well as necessity.[29]

For another example of technical work leaving behind, as it were, the law of what is, Simon cites Cocteau's quip that photography has liberated painting. Painters no longer have to "imitate" or "represent" nature. They can now paint any way they want, and we are still drawn to admire their product.[30] But aesthetics being such a controversial subject, perhaps we should here add another example by a fiercely political author. In a pamphlet entitled *To Hell with Culture*, Sir Herbert Read predicts the coming of the revolution and the establishment of a Democratic Civilization and Democratic Culture, greater than any in history. But on his calmer pages, he also explains the power of art as follows:

> A song by Shakespeare or Blake, a melody by Bach or Mozart, a Persian carpet or a Greek vase—such "forms," in the words of Keats, "tease us out of thought as does eternity." They tease us out of our human preoccupations—the theme of epic and drama and novel— and for a few brief seconds hold us suspended in a timeless existence. Such rare moments are beyond daily reality, supersocial and in a sense superhuman.[31]

Simon would readily agree that human art has such power. But always a realist, he does not want us to forget its basic limitation. Because it is the work of a mind inescapably tied to data supplied by physical nature, human art can never be pure creation. Even so, modern technology has given the artists novel and powerful ways to expand the range of their creativity, and Simon believes that a closer collaboration between fine arts and technology would not only make our environment more beautiful but would also help to modify the largely utilitarian orientation of the present-day technological "culture."[32] The main point here, however, is that by this extension of the technical work of the mind, Simon shows how Aristotle's "art," which sets us at ease with regard to things to be made, can also take us beyond the law of what is into the realm of free expansion and expression. Thus both intellectual and technical work, rightly pursued, have the power to fulfill the transcendental aspirations of a humanist and per chance democratic culture.

This leaves the question of the potential contribution to a humanist and democratic culture by the third kind of the works of the mind, namely, the moral and social work. Science and art, as Simon explains it, contribute to the culture capable of sustaining true leisure by blossoming into activities of free expansion. Should we, then, look for a kindred cultural contribution from the moral and social work of the mind? Can social work, too, transcend necessity in some way, as science and art do, to create a virtual reality of its own making? Are there counterparts to symbolic logic or surrealist painting in the construction of social reality? . . . Or is the literal meaning of *utopia* fixed forever?

In contrast to the ultimate feats of which science and art are capable, the social and moral work of the mind, Simon holds, does not aim or admit of any kind of transcendence. Prudence, to use its Aristotelian name, is always and strictly only about what is necessary and useful under given existential circumstances. This does not mean, of course, that our choices in "the construction of social reality" are uniquely determined. For instance, we may choose to drive either on the right side or on the left side of the road. But it is not just useful, it is absolutely necessary that, for the good of all, we choose one or the other side. In moral and social work, there is no point in looking for free expansion. Its aim must always remain one of legal fulfillment, lest its purpose be subverted.[33] Or to put it in another way, problems of action can never be solved by the intellectual, technical, or artistic work of the mind. Politics remains forever the work of prudence, whose reasoning is guided by good will.

The history of the twentieth century has provided ample evidence that the wholesale pursuit of any kind of utopia must be fatal to decent politics. Yet the ideologies that support various forms of government have always embodied lesser illusions, whose harm is avoided by inconsistent practice. Thus as noted in chapter 3, historical liberalism subscribes to an illusory deficiency theory of government that attributes the need for political authority basically to the contingencies of life and human weakness, if not also wickedness. But as Simon establishes convincingly, the truth of the matter is that the need for authority is generated by liberty which, in turn, is made possible by authority.[34] The specifically democratic "political process," as we have seen, sets no limits to the potential cooperation between liberty and authority. Except that their cooperation requires a matching amount of social and moral work.

WORK AND DEMOCRACY

We must begin by noting that the ancient Greeks are by no means the only ones who deny that politics is work. The most famous modern celebrants of work do the same, albeit for reasons of their own. The reason why politics, and culture, were held to be something special in "classical" societies is hardly a mystery. The ruling elites insisted on it, and believed it, not just because they did not want to share power with the masses but also because those illiterate masses were simply not up to it. But when the advocates of "people's power" and the spokesmen for the victorious middle class also want to deny that politics is a species of work, a more elaborate explanation is called for. This modern denial may well be in part a reaction against the history-long royal and aristocratic monopolization and glorification of politics. Visions of anarchy would be a natural response following centuries of authoritarian exploitation. But that cannot be the whole answer, and a realistic assessment of democratic prospects in the twenty-first century requires this paradox to be solved.

As noted above, the "classical" Greek thinkers present politics as an activity that is not just superior but differs from work in kind. This difference is grandly featured in the *Republic* of Plato, where the strict social division between the guardians and the producers is justified by the myth which describes them as being cast of different metals. Aristotle does not go for myths, but he, too, reserves politics only for those with natural aptitude for it and relegates work in effect to the "slaves by nature." And two millennia after Plato and Aristotle, a major modern writer would still insist that "the occupation of a hairdresser, or a candle maker, cannot be a matter of honor to any person, to say nothing of a number of other, even more servile employments." "Such description of men," Edmund Burke explains, "ought not to suffer oppression from the state; but the state suffers oppression, if such as they, either individually or collectively, are permitted to rule."[35] In other words, through most of history work was held to be a "servile occupation," and freedom from its "fetters" was considered the necessary basis of politics as well as of culture. And given the old predemocratic social order, this belief was no less self-evident to the common working people than it was to their "betters" and rulers.

But all that has now changed. Not only do hairdressers, the modern counterparts of candle makers, and the rest of the members of the "working classes" participate in the politics of most countries, but few today would consider politics a leisure activity. To organize elections, make laws, and run the government (especially when it is done "businesslike") is clearly not a pastime, and most people will grant that like everyone else politicians should be paid for what they do. In short, what is conventionally described as the democratic political "process" is in fact a complex product of deliberate activities by a large number of people. These people all know that they are working. But interestingly enough, the notion of politics as work is rejected by the two social theorists who have had the greatest influence in shaping modern political developments. Adam Smith and Karl Marx both explicitly deny that politics is a necessary, rational, useful activity. And in their wake, not many democratic theorists have been inclined to defend politics as moral and social work of the mind.

In contrast to what the ancient Greeks thought, and taught, both Smith and Marx take work, rather than politics, to be the highest human activity. And just as Plato and Aristotle denigrate work as less than a fully human operation, Smith and Marx look at politics either as a parasitic activity or as a fungible by-product of economics. Thus, as Hannah Arendt puts it, while Adam Smith makes work the source of all wealth, Marx turns it into the expression of the very humanity of man.[36] And at the same time, while Smith dismisses government and politics in the free-market society as unproductive, if not sheer waste, Marx again goes a step further and predicts that in the ideal communist society government and politics would simply wither away.[37] But the events of the twentieth century especially, not to cite the rest of history, have proved both Marx and Smith spectacularly wrong. It is one of the sadder ironies of history that the peoples of Russia, after overcoming communist delusions, are now rediscovering that free markets do not necessarily make for democracy. The lesson they are learning the hard way is not only that, contrary to both Marx and Smith, a regime is not defined by its economics; they are now also painfully aware that just writing a democratic constitution is not enough to secure domestic tranquillity and the blessings of liberty for all.[38] And in the West, despite their free enterprise rhetoric, even the most ardent champions of democratic capitalism versus the state know perfectly well that the system could not last a day, let alone prosper, without political support, which requires dedicated political work.[39]

Because what is at issue here is not whether work or politics is more important but rather whether politics *is* or is *not* work, and what kind of work, simply taking the Greek side, as it were, against Smith and Marx, only perpetuates confusion. For example, Hannah Arendt worries that the modern glorification of work (in pursuit of "the conquest of nature") may eventually bring about "the extinction of *vita activa*" (in pursuit of "the good for man"). And if the *animal laborans* wins, she writes, then "man will no longer be man."[40] Arendt is certainly right when she insists that "acting" and "making" need to be kept distinct in theory as well as in practice. The technological mind-set is bound to reduce freedom in social relations. Thus, warning against the pretenses of modern social sciences, Simon describes "social engineer" as "a mythological character in civilian clothes."[41] Doing and making differ with regard to their causal principles. The latter is a test of skills, the former a test of character. But that does not mean that politics, which depends ultimately on people's disposition, rather than on physical causes, is not and cannot be explained as a species of work. People have to work to acquire the right dispositions, and what they do once they have acquired these dispositions is also work—making necessary, rational, useful, decisions that continually modify the "political process" in which they participate.

All things considered, then, one may say that Simon's great accomplishment as a "philosopher in the city" consists precisely in his reconciling the modern discovery of the true scope of work in social life with the classical insight regarding the decisive role of politics in making that social life a good life. Though work may not be the very expression of our humanity, as Marx claims, there is no denying that man not only survives but also prospers by work, technical, social, and intellectual. Similarly, though Aristotle fails to recognize the kinship between manual work and the works of the mind, he is certainly right in holding that, man being a political animal by nature, the aim of politics must be "the good for man." But let us also note that despite his glorification of work, Marx is on record claiming that freedom begins only when work ends,[42] whereas Aristotle keeps the ranking of politics and philosophy in a sense open.[43] With his explication of the nature of work and the role of its varieties in human life, Simon consolidates all these views in a coherent account of modern developments, including the conditions for further democratic progress. By showing how intellectual and technical work may be left behind in the contemplation of truth and the admiration of beauty, Simon makes sense of Marx's admission that there is more to life than just work. And by identifying politics as the ultimate subject of the social and moral work of the mind, distinct from the technical and intellectual work, Simon also settles Aristotle's question about the rank of politics in relation to philosophy.

This reconciliation of ancient and modern insights, impressive as a theoretical feat, is also of considerable practical interest, because the question of the relation between politics and philosophy has been newly pressed by some contemporary theorists of democracy. For instance, as reported in chapter 2 above, Rorty and Rawls claim priority for democracy over "any search for an independent metaphysical or moral order."[44] Taking their commitment to democracy for granted, one is led to suspect that either their philosophy or their political theory, or both, must be wrong somewhere. For rather than by "refusing to hold reality and justice in the same vision" (Yeats/Rorty), the aspirations of democracy would seem to stand a better chance of being realized, as Simon argues, in a cultural environment "in which moral philosophy is no longer seen as the thing that threatens to cripple resolution and endanger society."[45] Before concluding with Simon's practical proposal how best to promote such an environment, it will be useful to show how at least Rawls's and Rorty's good democratic intentions are redeemed by Simon's concept of politics as the subject of moral and social work.

Rorty is right when he insists on the priority of democracy over philosophy; in the real world, knowing reality is second to coping with it. And so is Rawls also right when he separates the need for a democratic overlapping political consensus from all metaphysical search for truth. Clearly, what they both want is to protect the existential democratic pursuit of life, liberty, and happiness from interference by the notoriously controversial philosophical speculations about what it all means. But if Aristotle is right that, always and everywhere, it is politics that "legislates what we are to do and what we are to abstain from," Rorty and Rawls, with best intentions, have gotten it all wrong. The useful truth is the other way around. For the sake of life, liberty, and the pursuit of happiness, it is democracy that must leave philosophy, and science, and art, alone. And the chances of that happening depend very much on the moral and social work invested in democratic politics.

As we have seen, Simon has no problem separating live politics from philosophical speculation. Theory is not of much use in dealing with specific contingent events. The answer of what to do in given, unique social and moral situations cannot be derived logically from any general premises. Whether to do this, or to abstain from that, here and now, is always a "judgment call." Simon calls it the ultimate practical judgment and explains at length that in that judgment reason is guided by good will.[46] There is thus nothing necessarily wrong with claiming the priority of prudence, or of politics, or of democracy over philosophy in facing specific, unique real life problems. But that does not mean that asserting this priority cannot get out of control at the expense not only of philosophy but also of democracy itself. Recall the trial of Socrates.

In the wrong hands, democracy can be the worst of regimes. To be the best, democracy needs a lot of social and moral work.

What democracy clearly needs is enough people to do the right thing as ordinary citizens as well as public officials. But for anyone to be able to do that requires preparation, which Simon accurately defines as moral and social work. To become a temperate, courageous, just, and prudent person, who will not shirk civic duty and will not abuse power, requires much effort and continuous practice. But is it not clear that only the people who have acquired these personal and civic virtues of temperance, courage, justice and prudence are those who can be expected to work out an overlapping political consensus that recognizes in what sense democracy comes before philosophy—and leaves philosophy alone. But equally uncomfortable with the notion of moral virtues as with the notion of common good, in their defense of the autonomy and the existential priority of politics, Rorty and Rawls are forced to settle in effect for second-rate democracy. Their overlapping political consensus, reminiscent of the old "social contracts," is a product of selfish utilitarian calculations by morally unencumbered individuals. It is not the free choice of responsible citizens. Free to go either way, their individuals consent, as Aristotle might put it, for the sake of sheer life rather than good life.

A REALIST VIEW OF PROGRESS

And so we come to the deepest truth about the prospects of democracy in the real world, and this truth has nothing to do with metaphysics. The reason why some have always thought democracy to be an inferior form of government is that they did not think the majority of the people capable either of ruling or even simply being responsible citizens. It is a delicate point, but the friends of democracy must not overlook the lessons of American history. The civil rights struggles endemic to United States politics have not always been against minority rule. Democracy in the real world does not work by solemn declarations and formal institutions. What the government of the people, for the people, and by the people needs above all is people who know that the competition of interests is not the last end of politics, and who are ready to do their share of the social and moral work needed to keep democratic liberty and democratic authority working together. Democracy can survive only if its political process includes enough such people. But contrary to some early modern enthusiasts for democracy, and many current champions of its promise, there is no guarantee that the vastly improved material conditions of modern life, which include extended leisure time, will necessarily reduce social problems, or induce democratic citizens to take an unselfish interest in politics. Thus Plato's and Toqueville's comments on the risks of a democratic regime, cited at the end of the last chapter, must remain a valid concern. But even as the debates over the various requirements of democratic politics go on, there is one choice that may well make a difference for the future. Is the glass half empty or half full? For Simon, stressing the first alternative is more likely to support the right kind of approach to doing what still needs to be done.

Reflecting in the aftermath of the Second World War on what might be the best way to consolidate the victory and the prospects of democracy, Simon proposed what he called a pessimistic theory of progress. For him, the magnitude of that latest human tragedy—fifty million dead—only confirmed the history-long record of human weakness, foolishness, and misery, which makes a sad mockery of all forms of belief in the inevitable progress of mankind. But Simon also took care to distinguish his position from the pessimism of disillusioned optimists, who are prone to give up hope (and often make a show of it).[47] Half a century later, in a world that has in fact become not only more democratic but has also seen the narrowing of the gap between optimists and pessimists, I propose to rename Simon's theory a realistic theory of progress. Despite improvements, many new problems of global proportions have conspired to leave the human political condition as it has always been—without guarantees either against reversals or for further improvements. Even just to keep its gains, material and political, modern democratic society cannot afford to relax. And the chances of further democratic advances clearly require additional investment not only in intellectual and technical but above all in social and moral work. This is why Simon holds firmly that the attitude called work ethic has not been outdated. For one thing, culture depends on continuing progress in science and art, that is, intellectual and technical work. But it is politics that needs work the most. Democratic cooperation between liberty and authority requires an extraordinary amount and kind of social and moral work. Democratic citizens and leaders may on solemn occasions share the feeling that their communion links them to generations past and those yet to be born, but that is not a case of true "free expansion." Burke was right about the danger of abstract speculation in politics. The satisfaction of moral and social work does not come from the truth or beauty of one's own making. The reward of civic virtue can never be anything more than the satisfaction of "legal fulfillment," of a job well done. And that is why democratic politics needs people with a work ethic, and more of them than any other regime. To make liberty and authority work together on equal terms is a tough job. Simon believes it is important to say so, and he leaves us the following explanation:

> All that is essentially implied by moral *realism* is a perfectly sincere disposition to see the wrong and injustice wherever they appear, together with their frequency and extent; will and resolution to knock down the protective screens which our fear and our laziness manufacture to spare us the sight of evil; and a thorough sense of the immense difficulties which the accomplishment of good presents.

One could say that *realism* is nothing but depth of moral intelligence. In the life of study, what distinguishes really intelligent people from those who have only a brilliant appearance of intelligence is an ability to understand that the most trifling questions, once examined, will always turn out to be incomparably more difficult than one could have foreseen, to understand that any progress in the exploration of a question necessarily has the effect of making new difficulties apparent, difficulties greater than those already surmounted. Only shallow minds believe that there are such things as easy questions in the sciences, in philosophy, in history. Profound minds know that there are no easy questions. Yet they are not morose minds; they have accepted the law of difficulty which is the law of our intelligence; and to the cheap satisfactions obtained by brilliant and shallow minds they prefer the austere joys which accompany familiarity with mystery. Optimists are men who believe that one can easily be good, become better, improve mankind's lot: they are the shallow minds, the idiots, of the practical order.

Just as a profound scientific mind is not necessarily a morose mind, so a *realist* has no reason to be a sullen person. It is the disillusioned optimist who has good reasons for losing sight of the possibility of progress and the exigency of progress which are written in our nature: for him the practical solution is to let things go. But to the true *realist* this is an inadmissible solution. An exact knowledge of the wrong reveals the power of the good and arouses in our souls an uncompromising will to act and to struggle for the better world whose realization our nature, from the depth of its wretchedness, demands.[48]

NOTES

1. As Thorstein Veblen puts it, while the leisure classes throughout history were occupied "with government, warfare, religious observances, and sports," the great body of people had always been hard at work "to turn things to human use." *The Theory of the Leisure Class* (New York: Modern Library, 1934), p. 2; quoted by Simon in *Work, Society, and Culture* (New York: Fordham University Press, 1971, 1987), p. 58.

2. Edited by James C. Charlesworth (Philadelphia: American Academy of Political and Social Sciences, 1964.)

3. Sebastian de Grazia, *Of Time, Work, and Leisure* (New York: Twentieth Century Fund, 1962), p. 327.

4. Ibid., p. 379.

5. Ibid., p. 409.

6. Ibid., p. 434.

7. Chris Rojek, *Capitalism and Leisure Theory* (London: Sage Publications, 1983), pp. 8, 181.

8. Chris Rojek, *Decentering Leisure: Rethinking Leisure Theory* (London: Sage Publications, 1995).

9. Rojek writes: "By committing ourselves to decentering leisure we emancipate leisure from the modernist burden of *necessarily* connoting freedom, choice, life satisfaction and escape with leisure. We recover what the illusions of modernity have concealed." Ibid., p. 192.

10. Joseph Pieper, *Leisure: The Basis of Culture* (New York: Pantheon, 1952), p. 56.

11. Ibid., 64–65.

12. Ibid., 70–71.

13. The English title was suggested to Pieper by T. S. Eliot. The original German title of Pieper's monograph is *Musse und Kult*, "Leisure and Worship." In his *Notes Toward the Definition of Culture* (New York: Harcourt, Brace, 1949), Eliot argues, similarly to de Grazia, that those who produce and maintain culture should be allowed by society to specialize in it.

14. See Simon, *Work, Society, and Culture*, p. 182.

15. *Republic* 9.590; *Metaphysics* 1.1.981b23; 1.1.981a24; quoted in *Work, Society and Culture*, p. 145.

16. *Plutarch's Lives* (New York: Modern Library, 1932), p. 183; quoted in *Work, Society, and Culture*, p. 2.

17. *Work, Society, and Culture*, pp. 26, 183. Kant (1724–1804), Simon adds, "no longer wrote for society people but rather for professional philosophers and serious students of philosophy."

18. *Work, Society, and Culture*, p. 85.

19. *Work, Society, and Culture*, p. 158. According to Simon, Aristotle expounds this theory in book six of *Ethics*, and in *Analytica Posteriora*. But since the treatment in the latter gives the impression that culture is an abstract theoretical achievement, Simon leaves it out.

20. *Work, Society, and Culture*, p. 159ff. For the difference between habitus and virtue see above, chapter 2.

21. *Work, Society, and Culture*, pp. 5–10.

22. See Simon's "The Concept of Work," in *Works of the Mind*, ed. Robert B. Heywood (Chicago: University of Chicago Press, 1947, 1966), pp. 3–17; the essay is included in *Philosopher at Work*, ed. Anthony O. Simon (Lanham, MD: Rowman & Littlefield, 1999),

23. "Those who refuse to make a preliminary judgement that the faculty of knowing has a certain indefectibility, while readily proclaiming that it can be deprived of it, are starting in the wrong direction. They want to proceed without telling anyone the conditions on which their interpretation of knowledge will avoid being contradictory." *Metaphysics of Knowledge* (New York: Fordham University Press, 1990), p. 38.

24. "The Concept of Work," p. 9. Elsewhere, Simon quotes John of St. Thomas: "Understanding is not exactly like a passage, or the ordinary production of some term or effect. Rather, it is a perfection ultimately intended by the intellect, and if it does have some effect, that effect is ordered to its own good. The perfection of the intellect consists, not in producing an effect, but in attaining truth; and if it produces any effect, e.g., the concept, it is for the sake of contemplating the truth in it, and so the contemplation is what finally actuates and perfects the intellect. Thus the supreme perfection of the intellect consists in actual understanding and contemplation." *Metaphysics of Knowledge*, p. 135n54.

25. "The Concept of Work," p. 16.

26. *Work, Society, and Culture*, p. 12. See also *Metaphysics of Knowledge*, "Motionless Activity," pp. 71–73.

27. "Some activities embody the idea of compliance with a law, while others are thought to be free. For the first type, I have coined the expression *activities of legal fulfillment*, in which the adjective 'legal' refers not to a statute but to law in the broadest possible sense. I call the second type *activities of fee development*." *Work, Society, and Culture*, p. 24.

28. Ibid., p. 172. Simon explains that while by "nature" we mean something definite, "when we say 'rational,' we posit a nature which over and above its definite needs enjoys an openness to infinity." Ibid., p. 169.

29. See Simon, "Art and Morality," in *The New Scholasticism*, vol. 35, no. 3 (1961), pp. 338–41.

30. *Work, Society, and Culture*, p. 178.

31. Herbert Read, *To Hell with Culture* (London: Routledge and Keagan Paul, 1963), p. 35. "The whole of our capitalist culture is one immense veneer," he writes, "a surface refinement hiding the cheapness and shoddiness at the heart of things. To hell with such culture! To the rubbish-heap and furnace with it all." P. 30.

32. "As a general rule, the more powerful the technique at his disposal, the greater the possibilities for creative choices open to any worker. I believe that once these creative possibilities are fully recognized, modern technology, traditionally held hostile to artistic refinement, could become an important contributing factor to the development of a truly humanist culture." *Work, Society, and Culture*, pp. 187–88.

33. *Work, Society, and Culture*, pp. 173–75.

34. See above, p. 69.

35. *Reflections on the Revolution in France*, ed. Thomas H.D. Mahoney (New York: Liberal Arts Press, 1955), p. 56.

36. According to Arendt, "The sudden rise of labor from the lowest, most despised position to the highest rank, as the most esteemed of human activities, began when Locke discovered that labor is the source of all property. It followed its course when Adam Smith asserted that labor was the source of all wealth and found its climax in Marx's 'system of labor,' where labor became the source of all productivity and the expression of the very humanity of man." *The Human Condition* (Chicago: University of Chicago Press, 1958), p. 101.

37. "The whole, or almost the whole public revenue, is in most countries employed in maintaining unproductive hands." Adam Smith, *The Wealth of Nations* (New York: Modern Library, 1937), p. 325. "The government of persons is replaced by the administration of things" and the state "withers away." Friedrich Engels, *Anti-Dühring* (New York: International Publishers, 1939), p. 115.

38. The post-communist situation in the former Soviet Union is discussed by Robert V. Daniels in *Russia's Transformation: Snapshots of a Crumbling System* (Lanham, MD: Rowman and Littlefield, 1998). See also David Remnick, *Lenin's Tomb* (New York: Random House, 1993).

39. See Michael Novak, *The Fire of Invention: Civil Society and the Future of the Corporation* (Lanham, MD: Rowman and Littlefield, 1997). Novak claims that "the overpromising . . . and overreaching state" of the twentieth century has brought about "a pronounced decline in morals and morale, a growing under-

class, and a return to serfdom." But in what sometimes reads as a deliberate put-on, looking forward in "bright Alpine sunlight," he praises the business corporation as "today's leading revolutionary force," whose most important effect "is to raise the poor out of poverty and to offer unparalleled opportunities for the development of human talents." pp. 117, 119.

40. Arendt, *Human Condition*, p. 322.

41. "The Concept of Work," p. 8. See also above, p. 40.

42. "Das Reich der Freiheit beginnt in der Tat erst da, wo das Arbeiten . . . aufhört." *Das Kapital*, ch. 48. Quoted in Arendt, *The Human Condition*, p. 87n.

43. "Let us now address those who, while they agree that the life of virtue is most eligible, differ about the manner of practicing it." *Politics* 7.3. 1325ª17. Aristotle's argument, summarized in the table of contents of the Jowett translation, is as follows: "A virtuous life implies activity, but activity may be speculative as well as practical. Those are wrong who regard the life of a practicing politician as degrading. But again they are wrong who treat political power as the highest good."

44. See pp. 26–27.

45. See above, p. 43.

46. *Practical Knowledge*, pp. 17–18.

47. "When a man calls attention to himself by the bitterness, the snarling tone, of his criticism of modern errors, the aberrations of his contemporaries, the stupidity of the majority, the increasingly rapid decadence of our civilization," etc., Simon writes, it is because he has in his mind a model of harmony "immeasurably purer than even the best experience has the slightest chance of showing him." *Community of the Free*, p. 103.

48. *Community of the Free*, pp. 120–21. The present text is a slighlty edited version of the original.

BIBLIOGRAPHY

BY YVES R. SIMON

Introduction à l'ontologie du connaître. Paris: Desclée de Brouwer, 1934. *An Introduction to Metaphysics of Knowledge,* trans. Vukan Kuic and Richard J. Thompson. New York: Fordham University Press, 1990.

Critique de la connaissance morale. Paris: Desclée de Brouwer, 1934.

"Le problème de la transcendance et le défi de Proudhon," in *Nova et Vetera* (Geneva), Vol. 9 (1934); English translation by Charles P. O'Donnell and Vukan Kuic in *Thought,* Vol. 54, No. 1 (1979).

La campagne d'Éthiopie et la pensée politique française. Paris: Desclée de Brouwer, 1936.

"Notes sur le fédéralisme proudhonnien," in *Esprit* (Paris), No. 5 (April 1937); English translation by Vukan Kuic in *Publius,* Vol. 3, No. 2 (1973).

Trois leçons sur le travail. Paris: Pierre Téqui, 1938.

Nature and Functions of Authority. Milwaukee, WI: Marquette University Press, 1940.

La grande crise de la République Française. Montreal: Éditions de l'Arbre, 1941. *The Road to Vichy,* trans. James A. Corbett and George J. McMorrow. New York: Sheed and Ward, 1942; reprinted with new introduction by John Helman at University Press of America, Lanham, MD, 1988.

La Marche à la délivrance. New York: Éditions de la Maison Française, 1942. *The March to Liberation,* trans. Victor M. Hamm. Milwaukee, WI: The Tower Press, 1942.

"Thomism and Democracy," in *Science, Philosophy, and Religion: Second Symposium,* ed. Louis Finkelstein and Lyman Bryson. New York: Conference on Science, Philosophy and Religion in Their Relation to the Democratic Way of Life, Inc., 1942.

"Maritain's Philosophy of the Sciences," in *The Thomist,* Vol. 5 (1943); reprinted in *The Philosophy of Physics,* ed. Vincent E. Smith. New York: St. John's University Press, 1961.

Prévoir et savoir: Études sur l'idée de nécessité dans la pensée sientifique et en philosophie. Montreal: Éditions de l'Arbre, 1944; English translation, *Foresight and Knowledge*, by Ralph Nelson and Anthony O. Simon. New York: Fordham University Press, 1995.

Par delà l'expérience du désespoir. Montreal: Lucien Parizeau, 1945. *The Community of the Free*, trans. Willard R. Trask. New York: Henry Holt, 1947; reprinted at University Press of America, Lanham, MD, 1984.

"The Concept of Work," in *The Works of the Mind*, ed. Robert B. Heywood. Chicago: The University of Chicago Press, 1947, 1966: reprinted in *A Philosopher at Work*, ed. Anthony O. Simon. Lanham, MD: Rowman and Littlefield, 1999.

La civilisation Américaine, ed. Yves R. Simon. Paris: Desclée de Brouwer, 1950.

Philosophy of Democratic Government. Chicago: The University of Chicago Press, 1951, 1961, 1977; reprinted at University of Notre Dame Press, Notre Dame, IN, 1993.

Traité du libre arbitre. Liége: Sciences et Lettres, 1951. *Freedom of Choice*, trans. and ed. Peter Wolff. New York: Fordham University Press, 1969, 1987.

The Material Logic of John of St. Thomas, trans. Yves R. Simon, John J. Glanville, G. Donald Hollenhorst. Chicago: The University of Chicago Press, 1955.

"The Philosopher's Calling," in *Proceedings of the American Catholic Philosophical Association*. Washington, DC. Vol. 32 (1958); reprinted in *A Philosopher at Work*, ed. Anthony O. Simon. Lanham, MD: Rowman and Littlefield, 1999.

A General Theory of Authority. Notre Dame, IN: University of Notre Dame Press, 1962, 1980.

The Tradition of Natural Law, ed. Vukan Kuic. New York: Fordham University Press, 1965, 1992.

Freedom and Community, ed. Charles P. O'Donnell. New York: Fordham University Press, 1968.

The Great Dialogue of Nature and Space, ed. Gerard J. Dalcourt. Albany, NY: Magi Books, 1970.

Work, Society, and Culture, ed. Vukan Kuic. New York: Fordham University Press, 1971, 1987.

The Definition of Moral Virtue, ed. Vukan Kuic. New York: Fordham University Press, 1986, 1989.

Practical Knowledge, ed. Robert J. Mulvaney. New York: Fordham University Press, 1991.

NOTE: A complete up-to-date bibliography of Simon has been compiled by Anthony O. Simon and published with accompanying essays by several contributors in *Acquaintance with the Absolute: The Philosophy of Yves R. Simon*. New York: Fordham University Press, 1998.

SELECTED BIBLIOGRAPHY

Adler, Mortimer. *The Idea of Freedom*. 2 vols. Garden City, NY: Doubleday, 1958, 1961.

Arendt, Hannah. *Between Past and Future*. New York: Meridian Books, 1963.

————. *The Human Condition*. Chicago: The University of Chicago Press, 1958.

Aristotle. *The Basic Works of Aristotle*, ed. Richard Mckeon. New York: Random House, 1941.

Barnet, Richard, and John Cavanaugh. *Global Dreams: Imperial Corporations and the New World Order*. New York: Simon and Schuster, 1994.

Bay, Christian. *The Structure of Freedom*. Stanford, CA: Stanford University Press, 1958.

Bellah, Robert N., et al., eds. *The Habits of the Heart*. Berkeley, CA: University of California Press, 1996.

Berlin, Isaiah. *Four Essays on Liberty*. New York: Oxford University Press, 1969.

Bowles, Samuel, and Herbert Gintis. *Democracy and Capitalism: Property, Community and the Contradictions of Modern Social Thought*. New York: Basic Books, 1986.

Burke, Edmund. *Reflections on the Revolution in France*, ed. Thomas H. D. Mahoney. New York: Liberal Arts Press, 1955.

Burns, James MacGregor. *The Deadlock of Democracy*. Engelwood Cliffs, NJ: Prentice-Hall, 1963.

Charlesworth, James C., ed. *Leisure: A Blessing or a Curse?* Philadelphia: American Academy of Political and Social Sciences, 1964.

Cranston, Maurice. "Political Philosophy in Our Time," in *The Great Ideas Today*. Chicago: Encyclopedia Britannica, 1975.

Dahl, Robert A. *Democracy and Its Critics*. New Haven, CT: Yale University Press, 1989.

Daniels, Robert V. *Russia's Transformation: Snapshots of a Crumbling System*. Lanham, MD: Rowman and Littlefield, 1998.

De Grazia, Sebastian. *Of Time, Work, and Leisure*. New York: Twentieth Century Fund, 1962.

Delaney, C. F., ed. *The Liberalism-Communitarianism Debate*. Lanham, MD: Rowman and Littlefield, 1994.

Eddington, A. S. *The Nature of the Physical World*. New York: Macmillan, 1927.

Eliot, T. S. *Notes Toward the Definition of Culture*. New York: Harcourt, Brace, 1949.

Engels, Friedrich. *Anti-Dühring*. New York: International Publishers, 1939.

Etzioni, Amitai, ed. *Rights and the Common Good: The Communitarian Perspective*. New York: St. Martin's Press, 1995.

Hamilton, Alexander, John Jay, and James Madison. *The Federalist*. New York: Modern Library, n.d.

Hall, David A. *Richard Rorty: Prophet and Poet of the New Pragmatism*. Albany, NY: State University of New York Press, 1994.

Hancock, Curtis, and Anthony O. Simon, eds. *Freedom, Virtue, and the Common Good*. Notre Dame, IN: Notre Dame University Press, 1995.

Hayek, Friedrich. *The Constitution of Liberty*. Chicago: The University of Chicago Press, 1960.

Heidegger, Martin. *The Question Concerning Technology and Other Essays*, trans. W. Lowitt. New York: Harper, 1977.

Holmes, Stephen. *The Anatomy of Antiliberalism*. Cambridge, MA: Harvard University Press, 1993.

———. *Passions and Constraint: On the Theory of Liberal Democracy*. Chicago: The University of Chicago Press, 1995.

House, Vanden D. *Without God or His Double: Realism, Relativism, and Rorty*. Leiden, Netherlands: E. J. Brill, 1994.

James, William. *Psychology: The Briefer Course*, ed. Gordon Alport. New York: Harper Torch Books, 1952.

Kennedy, Eugene, and Sara C. Charles. *Authority: The Most Misunderstood Idea in America*. New York: Free Press, 1997.

Kolenda, Konstantin. *Rorty's Humanistic Pragmatism: Philosopy Democratized*. Tampa, FL: University of South Florida Press, 1990.

Kuttner, Robert L., ed. *Ticking Time Bombs: The New Conservative Assault on Democracy*. New York: New Press, 1996.

Laski, Harold. *Liberty in the Modern State*. New York: The Viking Press, 1949.

Levinson, Sanford. *Constitutional Faith*. Princeton, NJ: Princeton University Press, 1988.

Maritain, Jacques. *Science and Wisdom*. London: Geoffrey Bles, 1940.

Melzer, A. M., J. Weinberger, and M. R. Zinman, eds. *Technology in the Western Political Tradition*. Ithaca, NY: Cornell University Press, 1993.

Montesquieu. *The Spirit of Laws*, ed. D. W. Carrithers. Berkeley, CA: University of California Press, 1977.

Novak, Michael. *The Fire of Invention: Civil Society and the Future of the Corporation*. Lanham, MD: Rowman and Littlefield, 1997.

———. *The Spirit of Democratic Capitalism*. New York: American Enterprise Institute, 1986.

Paine, Thomas. *The Writings of Thomas Paine*. New York: G. P. Putnam's Sons, 1894.

Pieper, Joseph. *Leisure: The Basis of Culture*. New York: Pantheon, 1952.

Plato. *The Republic*, trans. Desmond Lee. New York: Penguin Books, 1974.

Rawls, John. "Justice as Fairness: Political Not Metaphysical," *Philosophy and Public Affairs*, Vol. 14, No. 3 (1985), pp. 223–51.

———. *A Theory of Justice*. Cambridge, MA: Harvard University Press, 1971.

———. "The Priority of Right and Ideas of the Good" in *Philosophy and Public Affairs*, Vol. 17, No. 3 (1988), pp. 251–76.

Read, Herbert. *To Hell with Culture*. London: Routledge and Keagan Paul, 1963.

Reichenbach, Hans. *The Rise of Scientific Philosophy*. Berkeley, CA: University of California Press, 1951.

Remnick, David. *Lenin's Tomb*. New York: Random House, 1993.

Rodrick, Dani. *Has Globalization Gone Too Far?* Cambridge, MA: Harvard University Press, 1996.

Rojek, Chris. *Capitalism and Leisure Theory*. London: Sage Publications, 1983.

———. *Decentering Leisure: Rethinking Leisure Theory*. London: Sage Publications, 1995.

Rourke, Thomas R. *A Conscience as Large as the World: Yves R. Simon versus the Catholic Neoconservatives*. Lanham, MD: Rowman and Littlefield, 1997.

Rorty, Richard. "The Priority of Democracy to Philosophy," in *The Virginia Statute for Religious Freedom*, ed. Merrill D. Preston and Robert C. Vaughan. Cambridge: Cambridge University Press, 1988.

Ryan, Alan, ed. *The Idea of Freedom: Essays in Honor of Isaiah Berlin*. New York: Oxford University Press, 1979.

Sandel, Michael. *Democracy's Discontent: America in Search of Public Philosophy*. Cambridge, MA: Belknap Press of the Harvard University Press, 1996.

Searle, John. *The Construction of Social Reality*. New York: Free Press, 1995.

Simon, Paule. "The Papers of Yves R. Simon," in *The New Scholasticism*, Vol. 32, No. 4 (1963).

Skinner, B. F. *Beyond Freedom and Dignity*. New York: Knopf, 1971.

Smith, Adam. *The Wealth of Nations*. New York: Modern Library, 1937.

Tocqueville, Alexis. *Democracy in America*. New York: Alfred A. Knopf, 1945.

Veblen, Thorstein. *The Theory of the Leisure Class*. New York: Modern Library, 1934.

Wolff, Edward N. *Top Heavy: The Increasing Inequality of Wealth in America and What Can Be Done about It*. New York: Twentieth Century Fund, 1996.

INDEX

ABOUT THE AUTHOR

VUKAN KUIC is Distinguished Professor Emeritus in the Department of Government and International Studies at the University of South Carolina. He earned his doctoral degree at the University of Chicago, where he took several courses with Yves R. Simon. He is the editor of three of Simon's posthumous volumes, *The Tradition of Natural Law, Work, Society, and Culture,* and *The Definition of Moral Virtue,* and co-translator with Richard J. Thompson of Simon's *Metaphysics of Knowledge.* His articles on a variety of subjects have appeared in *The Review of Politics, The Political Science Reviewer, The American Bar Association Journal, Publius, Chronicles,* and other publications.